BRITAIN IN OLD PHOTOGRAPHS

SOUTHAMPTON SINCE 1945

TONY GALLAHER

SUTTON PUBLISHING LIMITED

Sutton Publishing Limited
Phoenix Mill · Thrupp · Stroud
Gloucestershire · GL5 2BU

First published 1998

Copyright © Tony Gallaher, 1998

Cover photographs: (front) High Street, 1950;
(back) Demolition of Arundel Towers, 1997;
Title page photograph: Tudor House Museum.

British Library Cataloguing in Publication Data
A catalogue record for this book is available from the
British Library.

ISBN 0-7509-16966

Typeset in 10/12 Perpetua.
Typesetting and origination by
Sutton Publishing Limited.
Printed in Great Britain by
Ebenezer Baylis, Worcester.

Titanic Memorial, 1997. No book on Southampton would be complete without a mention of one of the city's greatest tragedies. The White Star liner *Titanic*, having set sail from Southampton on her maiden voyage, struck an iceberg and sank with the loss of over 1,500 lives in April 1912. The memorial in East Park is to the ship's engineers who remained at their stations for as long as possible while the ship was evacuated. In doing so they sacrificed their own lives to save the lives of others.

CONTENTS

Introduction   5

1.   The City Centre   7

2.   Down by the Docks   57

3.   To the East   69

4.   To the North   87

5.   To the West   107

6.   Across the River   117

     Acknowledgements   126

Holy Rood Church, 1997. The present Holy Rood Church replaced a medieval church on the same site in the 1840s. The church was all but destroyed in a German air raid on 30 November 1940 and lay derelict until the 1960s when the site was dedicated to the many merchant seamen that had lost their lives in the Second World War. The church also became well known in other ways before being dedicated to the Merchant Navy. Probably the most notable incident was when, in 1862, a chunk of masonry dislodged itself from the main building and crashed on to the crowds assembled below. No one was injured in the accident but a brass cross still marks the spot where the stones landed.

INTRODUCTION

This book is about the changes that have occurred in Southampton since the end of the Second World War. All changes cannot be attributed to the war but, like many other British cities, Southampton was very badly damaged. The docks, the railways and the Supermarine Works at Woolston, where the first Spitfire fighter planes were built, were among the primary targets for the enemy. However, much of the medieval heart of the city was destroyed, taking with it much of Southampton's ancient history. Many residential areas were also destroyed, depriving ordinary citizens of their homes.

Rebuilding began almost immediately after the war, starting with the rehousing of bombed-out inhabitants in prefabricated buildings, known as 'prefabs', on the (then) outskirts of the city such as Dale Valley Road and Harefield. The Above Bar Street, East Street and High Street shopping and commercial centres were rebuilt in the early 1950s in an austere post-war style of architecture owing to a lack of imagination by the city planners and a lack of government funds and materials for post-war redevelopment.

The prefabs were not built to last forever, and by the start of the 1950s work had begun on rehousing bombed-out inhabitants in permanent accommodation. Such rebuilding brought the Millbrook, Harefield and Thornhill housing estates into the city boundaries, with Millbrook being the last to join in 1954.

In the 1950s it was fairly easy to travel around Southampton by public transport. The old tramcar system went out of service on 31 December 1949 and the bus service that replaced it was just as efficient, if less nostalgic. In 1954 it was possible to catch a no. 5 bus in Kendal Avenue, Millbrook, and travel all the way around the city, without changing bus, to end up at the Floating Bridge in Woolston. It took over an hour, but it could be done and it was quite a pleasant ride.

However, with so many people living on the outskirts of the city, instead of residing in the centre as they once did, the strain on the road systems into and out of the city worsened over the years. That, combined with the unprecedented increase in private transport, has led to much of the major redevelopment in the city since the end of the Second World War. People need roads to get them in and out of the city, and also places to park their cars when they arrive at their destinations. It is this that has caused so many extensive changes to Southampton in recent years.

Despite the damage that was done by the Germans, the medieval street plan remained virtually intact in 1945. However, in several acts of misguided redevelopment, the city street plan was changed beyond recognition in an effort to ease the flow of traffic. Castle Way (part of the Inner Ring Road) was the result of the first such act; it cut a swath through the old city wall, taking with it much of bomb-damaged, although historic, French Street, as well as the virtually undamaged Portland Terrace. Thankfully the Regency buildings in Portland Terrace were allowed to remain, but the residential areas between Portland Terrace and the Western Esplanade fell victim to the planner's axe and were demolished. East Street was cut in half as a result of the demolition of the area around Orchard Lane and the creation of the Queensway part of the Inner Ring Road. A small alley known as Briton Street was widened to many times its original size to cater for the increase in traffic that resulted from the construction of the Inner Ring Road. That act also caused the demolition of several more ancient buildings that had survived the bombing.

Other recent road-improvement schemes in the city centre have caused the demise of the old Six Dials and the pretty Rose Gardens outside the Civic Centre. The Portswood, Swaythling and Bitterne areas of the city have been altered forever by their own traffic-improvement schemes.

Residential areas such as Northam and Chapel, where the houses were not the best of dwellings but the people had a unique community spirit, were swept away in the 1960s and 1970s, together with many of the older parts of Shirley and Bitterne. The Woolston area saw radical changes in 1977 when the long-awaited Itchen Bridge replaced the old Floating Bridge, while at the same time other parts of the city were also witnessing comprehensive changes.

This book shows some of the many changes that came about as a result of the Second World War. In some cases it shows how the streets looked in the years immediately after the Second World War and how they looked in 1997. With recent and contemporary photographs, the book goes on to show how things changed owing to later redevelopment of the city. Photographs of the city in the 1950s, 1960s and 1970s are compared with 1997 photographs to show many places with which Sotonians were once so familiar, but which have since disappeared without trace.

I have tried not to dwell entirely upon the scenes in the city centre; knowing that many Sotonians have fond memories of their roots, I have included several scenes from back streets in Chapel, Northam, Shirley and other districts. Many of the streets depicted may be familiar only to the people who lived or worked in the areas but they serve as useful reminders of how things were. I have also included photographs of the two major hospitals, as well as photographs of the four major shopping areas outside the city centre. Those four centres, Portswood, Shirley, Woolston and Bitterne, are well represented in this book.

The year 1997 saw some far-reaching changes in the city's landscape as plans for the Southampton of the future were put into action. Demolition of the buildings to the west of Above Bar Street, including buildings in Portland Terrace and the Western Esplanade, began in October 1997.

The overall plan is to open up the westward view towards the massive redevelopment that is to take place on the site of the old Pirelli cable factory. The new development will contain shopping malls, cafés, restaurants, pubs, car parks and all the other amenities associated with a big city's shopping centre. The demolition of the buildings between the Above Bar shopping precinct and the new development is expected to draw people to the new shops and transfer the focal point of the city to the west.

For hundreds of years, however, the focal point of the city has been the Bargate. Even the bombing of the Second World War could not alter that. All commercial development radiated from that old building from medieval times until the present day. I will not say that it is impossible to suddenly change such a focal point but I wonder if the new development will work. I would hate to see the busy area around the Bargate become a 'ghost town' after so many centuries.

Southampton has seen many changes over the years. It has always taken such changes in its stride and the people have adapted accordingly. Always a busy seaport, the city was important in the wool and wine trade in medieval times. When that trade dropped off the city became a major spa resort, but when that business fell out of popularity the railways had arrived, and Southampton entered the most prosperous phase of its history.

The coming of the railway meant that the Southampton docks could be expanded and the city soon became the major passenger port of the country. The years that followed saw many famous passenger liners use the port. That period, which survived the Second World War, came to an end in the 1960s with the advent of cheap and reliable air travel.

After the demise of the liners, the city adapted to become a major container port for the (then) revolutionary container ships. A new container port was built to the west of the existing docks but, while the Western Docks survived as a base for cruise liners, the Eastern Docks went into a decline, ending up as the pleasing Ocean Village development of shops, houses, cinemas and marinas.

Signs of the future indicate that Southampton will eventually become a dedicated 'University City'. Most new leisure development is aimed at people in their late teens and early twenties; the Southampton Institute continues to expand on its present site and has already taken over the old Plummer Roddis department store in Above Bar Street. When Tyrrell & Green's store is relocated to its purpose-built new premises on the old Pirelli site, the Southampton Institute has plans to take over the old building. The campus of the Southampton Institute would then extend from St Andrews Road in the east to West Marlands Road in the west, and could also include some of East Park.

Southampton and its people have lived through many changes in the past. No doubt they will survive these changes too.

THE CITY CENTRE

*HIGH STREET, ABOVE BAR STREET,
EAST STREET AND THE OLD TOWN*

Above Bar Street, upper west side, c. 1950. This side of Above Bar Street was almost completely destroyed in the blitz of 1940. Several temporary shops were erected on the site and housed some famous names before they moved into more permanent premises. Such names included Van Allen for ladies' fashions, Rego for menswear, Singer for sewing machines and, of course, the Plummer Roddis department store. At the far end of the row of temporary shops was C & A Modes and the steel skeleton of its new building can be seen rising above the ruins of the original building. (Veal Collection.)

Above Bar Street, upper west side, 1997. The temporary shops were removed in the 1950s to make way for the (then) controversial Guildhall Square. Many local people were opposed to the plan to make the Guildhall visible from Above Bar Street, but the construction of the square went ahead just the same. C & A Modes can still be seen in the near distance, while in the foreground stands the former Plummer Roddis department store, which was rebuilt in 1958 and later taken over by the Southampton Institute. It was renamed Sir James Matthews House to honour a local benefactor on 28 October 1994.

Above Bar Street, upper east side, *c.* 1950. Tyrrell & Green's original department store was destroyed in the blitz. The temporary building that took its place opened in 1949 and was there until 1957 when the present building opened. The chemist's shop disappeared when the row of shops was redeveloped; the new premises were used by optician Hudson Verity. Woodhouse's furniture store was badly damaged in the blitz but managed to keep its business running in the patched-up ground floor. In the distance is the long-gone Prospect Place and Fleming Reid's Scotch Wool House with the Dolcis shoe shop next door. (Veal Collection)

Above Bar Street, upper east side, 1997. Tyrrell & Green's department store dominates the scene in 1997. Over the years the store expanded greatly and took over several of the new premises that had been erected on the site of Prospect Place. Woodhouse's furniture store was rebuilt in 1957 and was later taken over by Court's furnishers. The premises became a public house called the Goose and Granite in December 1996.

Above Bar Street, lower west side, *c.* 1953. The offices and printing works of the *Southern Evening Echo* were completely destroyed in the blitz of 1940. The newspaper, however, continued to bring news to the people of Southampton with little disruption, thanks to the help of its sister newspaper in Bournemouth. A brand-new, purpose-built office and printing works were erected in 1953: the photograph shows the building in course of construction. Other new buildings had already been opened. Gilbey's off-licence was among the first to be erected, while the Weaver to Wearer tailor was already advertising suits at £6 6s 0d ready for when its shop opened. (City Heritage Services)

Above Bar Street, lower west side, 1997. The *Southern Evening Echo* Office stands empty and boarded up awaiting the demolition that will open up the main shopping area to the new shopping facilities that are to be built on the old Pirelli site in the Western Esplanade. The office itself closed in 1996, the administrative and printing functions moving to Nursling where state-of-the-art computers are being put to use. The building was occupied very briefly by Millets, the camping and outdoor clothing firm, which accounts for the sign over the door.

Above Bar Street, looking south, 1955. By the time this photograph was taken the post-war building line here was well established. Buses and private cars were allowed to drive along the road (and would be for another fifteen years until the precinct came into existence) and in 1955 parking was permitted virtually anywhere along the road. As can be seen from the photograph, it didn't appear to cause too many problems: in those days there were fewer cars on the roads. The real problems for Southampton seem to have begun with the pedestrianization of Above Bar Street and the resultant diversion of traffic around the precinct. (City Heritage Services)

Above Bar Street, looking south, 1997. Apart from the lack of traffic, the buildings look almost the same as in the photograph taken in 1955. The occupants of the shops have changed many times over the years but the overall aspect is the same. Until 1995 the Information Bureau stood in a prominent position at the northern end of the precinct. However, the city council had it removed to out-of-the-way Civic Centre Road in 1995 to enhance the view towards the Bargate. They had forgotten about the trees they had planted years earlier, which continued to obscure the view.

Above Bar Street, c. 1955. The rebuilding of middle Above Bar Street included the replacement of the temporary premises that housed Parkhouse & Wyatt, W.H. Smith, Halfords and Freeman Hardy & Willis. The new buildings were set back from the road to allow a later road-widening scheme to take place unhindered. A long-standing jeweller in Southampton, Parkhouse & Wyatt's original shop was on the corner of Above Bar Street and Hanover Buildings. The company moved to its Above Bar address in 1933 when the east side of the Bargate was redeveloped. (Veal Collection)

Above Bar Street, 1997. Many of the shops in middle Above Bar Street have seen various tenants over the past forty years but the Parkhouse & Wyatt company still has premises on the site. The old Sussex Hotel was an early target for the planners: it was demolished soon after the top picture was taken. A new Sussex Hotel was built on the same site but closed down in 1967; the ground floor of the new building was incorporated into the line of shops, while the first floor became a Chinese restaurant.

Above Bar Street looking north, *c.* 1972. When the plans for rebuilding Southampton after the bomb damage were made in 1942, the planners had already envisaged a traffic-free area in the main shopping street. The new buildings in this part of Above Bar Street were deliberately built back from the original building line to enable the road to be widened quite considerably. The first attempt at pedestrianization of the street was in August 1971 when large concrete tubs were placed in strategic positions and filled with shrubs and flowers. The odd bench here and there let weary shoppers rest their feet. (Veal Collection)

Above Bar Street looking north, 1997. The Above Bar shopping precinct is now well established. The area was paved over permanently in the 1980s and has undergone several minor alterations and improvements since then. Note the difference in the shops: Sainsbury's supermarket has gone, as has Mac Fisheries and Vernon & Tear. Many of the major stores in the street have extended their premises into those of their neighbours so that the street now has the same shop fronts as any other large city in the country.

Above Bar Street, *c.* 1975. The Odeon Cinema was built on the sites of Scullard's Hotel and the Alexandra Theatre. Opening as the Regal Cinema in June 1934, the name changed to the Odeon in April 1945. The cinema closed for good in September 1993 and the building, together with the neighbouring Portland Arms building, was demolished. The Portland Arms closed as a pub in 1971, the building later being used as an employment agency. To the right of the cinema stands the original Above Bar Church, which was built in 1881 as the Church of Christ. The shop of Jackson the Tailor is in the right foreground of the photograph. (Veal Collection)

Above Bar Street, 1997. The Odeon Cinema and the old Portland Arms premises were replaced by a block of modern shops in 1994. To the right, Above Bar Church was rebuilt in 1979 and incorporated into the line of shops seen in the photograph. The premises of Jackson the Tailor had many other uses after Jackson closed down; it is now a greetings card shop.

Bargate, south side, c. 1957. Southampton's historic town gate has been photographed many times in the past. This particular photograph, however, shows part of the temporary structure that housed Maye's department store in the High Street. Maye's store was rehoused in a brand-new building on the same site but later taken over by the Owen Owen group. The large, bay-windowed building to the right of Maye's shop was Gatti's Restaurant, while the shop to the right of that was Winter & Worth, the men's outfitters. The boarded site just beyond the Bargate later became Bourne & Hollingsworth's fashion store. (Veal Collection)

Bargate, south side, 1997. Forty years on from the top photograph, the Bargate has changed little. The surrounding area, however, has changed greatly. Owen Owen's store closed down in 1994; the building now houses Argos and T.K. Maxx. Gatti's and Winter & Worth moved to new premises on, more or less, their old sites in about 1960 when the line of the buildings was straightened. Both businesses have since disappeared, while the former Bourne & Hollingsworth's premises are now occupied by Littlewood's store.

Bargate, north side, 1948. This depressing photograph just about sums up the mood of the whole country in the early years after the war – grim, austere and raining! Tramcars were still running around the Bargate, although their days were numbered and, unusually, a bus can be seen heading north around the Bargate. Buses were generally restricted to the routes that tramcars couldn't manage, and so this photograph may have captured the time of the changeover from tramcars to buses. The two cyclists, miserable as they look in the rain, must have been very depressed by the view of the war damage that lay ahead of them in Above Bar Street. (Southampton Archives Services)

Bargate, north side, 1997. After many years of pursuing the idea of a workable Bargate traffic system, the eastern side of the Bargate was pedestrianized in the early 1990s, diverting traffic around the western side. The whole scene looks much tidier than in the 1948 photograph, and it seems to work. Behind the Bargate, on the western side, modern buildings were erected in the 1960s while, on the eastern side, the most significant change has been the construction of the Bargate Centre shopping mall on the site of Cooper's Brewery.

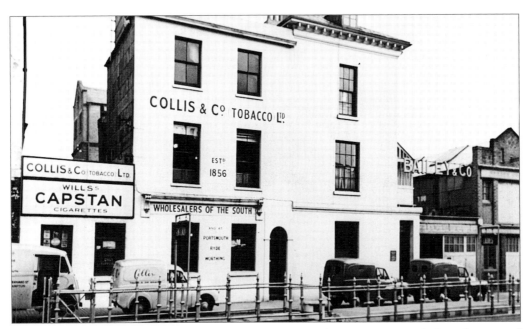

Bernard Street, north side, 1956. The premises of Collis & Company, the tobacconists, had stood in Bernard Street for many years, as had Bailey & Company, the builders. Many other smaller businesses also had their offices in this busy street. Behind the once elegant frontages, however, was a different scene: poor housing of the worst possible kind. In front of the buildings you can see the railings surrounding one of the foulest, subterranean public conveniences that ever existed in Southampton. It could not only be smelled from a mile away, but it was also home to many of the winos and vagrants in the area! (Southampton Archives Services)

Bernard Street, north side, 1997. The premises of Collis, Bailey and many other offices in the area, as well as the poor-quality housing behind them, were demolished just after the top photograph was taken. They were replaced by the St Bernard House flats, which were first occupied in 1958. On the right-hand side of St Bernard House, a new St James' Church was opened around the same time. That church, once Church of England, is now the Greek Orthodox Church of St Nicholas. The disgusting public conveniences, however, existed until well into the 1960s.

Bernard Street, north side, *c.* 1956. This side of Bernard Street, looking towards Holy Rood Church, was occupied by many small shops and businesses until the 1950s. Jeski's general store served many merchant seamen with their sea-going gear. Jeski specialized in providing merchandise for the ordinary crew members of the many liners that used Southampton as their home port, while Miller, Raynor & Haysom in Oxford Street kitted out those who were qualified, by one means or another, to wear stripes upon their sleeves. (Southampton Archives Services)

Bernard Street, north side, 1997. The shops on the corner of Orchard Lane and Bernard Street were demolished in the 1950s to make way for modern flats. The entrance to Orchard Lane was moved slightly to the west at the same time, which meant that St James House flats now straddle the old entrance into Orchard Lane. As can be seen from the present-day photograph, the area has changed beyond all recognition, although the Belisha beacons still stand on roughly the same spot as they did in the 1950s.

The Bird Aviary, *c.* 1955. Situated in the East Park since before the Second World War, the Bird Aviary was a popular attraction for many Southampton people. The aviary contained many different varieties of budgerigar, canary, parrot and cockatoo, as well as some of the rarer birds from our own country. The aviary stood just behind the memorial to the engineers of the ill-fated *Titanic*. It was also close to the pretty rock gardens and the unusually named 'Sugar Basin', which contained many meteorological instruments belonging to the Hudson Verity company. (Veal Collection)

Site of the Bird Aviary, 1997. Seen for some time by the city planners as being uneconomical, the Bird Aviary was demolished in the early 1990s, in spite of strong protests from many of the local people. Although it was an asset to the city, any local protests went unheeded and the site is now occupied by flower beds and a garden seat. The pretty rock garden, with its alpine plants and goldfish pond, still remains intact, but the interesting 'Sugar Basin' disappeared many years ago.

Brunswick Square, 1956. Once an elegant square of Victorian houses, Brunswick Square, hidden away in a side street off Bernard Street, was severely damaged during the war. The attractive row of terraced private houses was marred by an ugly gap left by the bombing and the area was virtually left to decay. People still lived in this once pleasant area in the years immediately after the Second World War, but by the 1960s the area was largely given over to commercial use. (Veal Collection)

Brunswick Square, 1997. Although still known as Brunswick Square, the Victorian houses have since been demolished to make way for the inevitable office blocks and car parks. No one lives in the area now but, as can be seen from the present-day photograph, as a business area it provides work for many people.

Bugle Street, *c.* 1955. The Duke of Wellington is Southampton's oldest public house. It stands in lower Bugle Street, one of the few major medieval streets left virtually intact after the war and the planners had altered the city. The building has been a pub since 1490, when it was known as the Brewe House and was run by Flemish brewer Rowland Johnson. It became known as the Shipwright's Arms in 1771 and received its present name in about 1815 to celebrate the Battle of Waterloo. The building was badly damaged during the wartime bombing of the city but was patched up and remained open for the duration. (City Heritage Services)

Bugle Street, 1997. At a cost of £34,407, the Duke of Wellington was completely rebuilt in 1961, reopening its doors to the drinking public in September 1963. Although it rightfully claims to be the oldest pub in the city – the medieval foundations are still intact – most of the structure of the pub is actually less than forty years old. Despite that fact, however, the pub still retains a certain old-world charm and atmosphere.

Castle Square, 1965. The infamous Juniper Berry public house stood on the left of the picture, while on the corner of Maddison Street was Magg's general store. In the background, between the buildings, is the funnel of a Union Castle liner alongside either 101 or 102 berth in the Western Docks. The Juniper Berry was a favourite haunt of the crews of the many liners that used Southampton and, while it was a good place for a night out, it was often the scene of trouble between the crews of rival ships. (Veal Collection)

Castle Square, 1997. Magg's general store and its neighbouring buildings disappeared in 1985 to make way for private dwellings. The pub, called the Bosun's Locker since 1993, no longer caters for merchant seamen on a run ashore because there are so few seamen now, as evidenced by the vacant berths in the Western Docks.

Civic Centre, *c.* 1970. When the Civic Centre was formally opened by the Duke of York in 1932, it was considered one of the most attractive civic buildings in the country. To enhance its image, the pretty rose gardens, with cherry trees and a fountain, the water of which changed colour at night, were laid out between the new Civic Centre Road and the Hants & Dorset bus station that stood opposite. Even when new the gardens must have been a welcoming sight for visitors to the city as they alighted from their buses. When mature, the gardens provided an air of relaxation and colour to an otherwise busy scene. (Southampton Archives Services)

Civic Centre, 1997. The Civic Centre itself looks much the same as it did over sixty years ago, but a busy dual carriageway and traffic system now run where the rose gardens and fountain once stood. The area has always been a busy one as far as traffic is concerned and the need for a road-widening scheme to ease the flow of traffic meant that the rose gardens had to go. They were ploughed over in 1987 when work on the new traffic system commenced. The fountain was preserved and now stands at the front of the Art Gallery on the other side of the building – I wonder if its water changes colour now.

East Street, looking west, *c.* 1950. This photograph must have been taken on a Sunday morning: apart from a solitary taxi, there is virtually no traffic to be seen and all the shops are closed except for Isaacs the newsagent's shop located next door to the St Mary's Hotel. Looking up East Street from the Central Hall, the first building on the right-hand side was Ganges boot factory. Next door to that was Southwell's baker's shop, while a few doors up from that was Curry's bicycle shop. Northover's butcher's shop was also on this side of the road, just before the bomb site that was once Edwin Jones' department store. (Veal Collection)

Site of East Street, looking west, 1997. It is now impossible to look up East Street from Central Hall. Thanks to redevelopment, that end of East Street was demolished in the early 1970s – the East Street Shopping Centre and Capital House offices being erected on the site. The Lime Street multi-storey car park was built at the same time and, in a forlorn attempt to compensate for the several public houses that disappeared in the redevelopment, the Royal Oak pub was built into the ground floor of the car park, almost as an afterthought.

East Street, looking east, c. 1950. The devastation that was East Street after the Second World War is more apparent from this photograph than from the one on the previous page. On the left, the ruins of Queens Buildings, otherwise known as Edwin Jones' department store, can be seen, while on the opposite side of the road all the little family run shops, pubs and cafés that once served this thriving and busy street have been flattened. For the first time in many years the spire of St Mary's Church can be seen towering above the ruins. (Veal Collection)

East Street, looking east, 1997. In 1997 the scene has changed beyond all recognition. Most of East Street was destroyed in the blitz of 1940 and what remained was, in turn, destroyed by the city planners. The Edwin Jones building was rebuilt in the 1950s and is now Debenham's department store, but the surviving old buildings at the eastern end of the street were demolished in the 1970s to make way for the East Street Shopping Centre. Another noticeable difference is Queensway running through the centre of the street making it, in effect, two quite different areas.

French Street, *c.* 1955. After the High Street, French Street was the second-most important street in medieval Southampton. The famous Southampton hymn writer, Isaac Watts, once lived in the street, which led from West Street to the Town Quay. The street was also famous for its breweries and many public houses: at one time in the 1860s there were over twenty pubs in the street! Like many other streets in the area, French Street was badly bombed during the war. One survivor was no. 58 (once the Bull's Head public house), which was badly damaged but still standing at the end of hostilities in 1945. (Veal Collection)

French Street, 1997. The development of Castle Way in the early 1960s wiped out most of French Street so that only a hundred yards or so of the original street remain. No. 58 still survives; after standing boarded up and derelict for many years, the building was taken over by English Heritage in 1984 and carefully restored to become one of the finest examples of fourteenth-century architecture in the country. Opened to the public in 1988, the building is now a museum that shows in detail how people lived in medieval times.

Grand Theatre, *c.* 1955. The Grand Theatre was built near the site of Marlands in 1898 and featured such performers as Henry Irving, Sarah Bernhardt and Lillie Langtry in its early years. Known as the New Hippodrome in the 1930s, the theatre closed in 1940 and reopened in December 1950. Although post-war cinema-going was still very popular during that period, the theatre just wasn't the success it had been. It ran dramas and concerts in an attempt to rekindle people's interests; in the 1950s the popular Harry Gold and his Pieces of Eight performed jazz concerts in the theatre on Sunday evenings. The theatre closed for good on 31 October 1959 and the building was demolished in March 1960. (Veal Collection)

Site of the Grand Theatre, 1997. Marlands House was built in the early 1960s on the site of the Grand Theatre and the original Lloyds Bank, which stood on the corner of Above Bar and Civic Centre Road. Lloyds Bank was rehoused in a modern building on the original site, where it remains to this day, while the rest of the modern block provided central premises for shops and offices. Just out of camera shot, on the right of the photograph, stood the old Hants & Dorset bus station, which was demolished to make way for the Marlands Centre in 1987.

Havelock Road, *c.* 1968. Nos 3 to 8 Havelock Road were still just about standing in 1968. The old buildings were badly damaged during the war and for many years afterwards they were held up by wooden props, although they were still used as offices. No. 3 was the Citizens' Advice Bureau, no. 4 was an estate agent, no. 5 was used by a midwife, no. 6 belonged to a motoring organization, no. 7 was a private house and no. 8 was used by a solicitor. The buildings were demolished shortly after this photograph was taken and the site lay empty for several years, being used as a temporary car park. (Rex Lancefield)

Havelock Road, 1997. Work began on redeveloping the Havelock Road site in 1990 and the futuristic Skandia House, which opened a year or two later, dominates the scene in 1997. The Inner Ring Road is to the left of the photograph, leading south to Portland Terrace. On the right the Civic Centre traffic system, with its many sets of traffic lights, controls the flow of traffic to the west, past the Central station and towards Mountbatten Way.

High Street, *c.* 1950. The western side of the High Street fared worse than the eastern side during the blitz of 1940. Most of the buildings on the once elegant western side were destroyed, while Lloyds Bank, the Star Hotel and the Dolphin Hotel on the eastern side remained more or less intact, even though damaged to some degree. The buildings in the left foreground of the photograph were also survivors of the blitz, but they did not survive the redevelopment plans of the city council – the whole row was later demolished and rebuilt in 1960s style. Only the National Provincial Bank on the corner of St Michaels Street survived the redevelopment because of its historic interest. (Veal Collection)

High Street, 1997. Taken overall, the view of this part of the High Street has changed very little since the 1950 photograph. The gap in the building line on the left was filled in during the late 1950s by a row of shops and offices that typified post-war austerity; although the shops have had many and varied tenants over the years, their fronts still look much the same today. A major change came in 1996 when the Woolwich Building Society office on the right became a pub called the Ferryman and Firkin.

High Street, *c.* 1956. German bombs laid waste to much of the lower High Street in 1940. To the left of the street can be seen Quilter's Vault, which miraculously remained standing, although the ancient Royal George Hotel which stood over the vault was completely destroyed, as were a dozen or more other ancient taverns in the area. Across the bombed sites can be seen St John's School and the spire of St Michael's Church, both of which, although damaged, somehow survived the bombing. Looking closer, you can see a couple of cars parked in what was then Broad Lane. (Veal Collection)

High Street, 1997. The photograph taken in 1997 shows very little difference in the area. The bombing of the city exposed many medieval foundations and vaults, which became the subject of important archaeological research. Many of the vaults are behind a high fence, but they can be seen from a viewing platform halfway along. Quilter's Vault still looks much the same as in the earlier photograph, but Castle House and the Marconi offices are now visible behind the trees. Broad Lane has since disappeared and Castle Way passes over the former bombed sites just to the north, on its way to Briton Street.

High Street, west side, *c.* 1950. The western side of the upper end of the High Street fared worse than the eastern side during the German bombing of 1940. The 1950 photograph shows how the view to St Michael's Church was opened up after the destruction of many ancient buildings on the western side. Many businesses were run from premises in this part of the High Street, including ship chandlers, insurance brokers, cafés and pubs, as well as numerous little shops. All such businesses were destroyed, many never to return to the area. (City Heritage Services)

High Street, west side, 1997. The western side of the High Street was rebuilt in the austere style that was typical of architecture in the late 1950s. The only survivor of the blitz in that area, the Leeds Permanent Building Society, located on the corner of the High Street and Castle Lane, was completely rebuilt in the 1950s and remained on the site until just a few years ago when the building was taken over by bookmaker William Hill.

High Street, west side, *c.* 1950. The Audit House was the forerunner of the Civic Centre, being the place where the town council met. The original Audit House was built in the fifteenth century and stood in the middle of the High Street opposite Holy Rood Church. That building became an obstruction to traffic and was demolished in the middle of the eighteenth century; a new Audit House was erected not far away on the western side of the High Street. After the blitz of 1940, all that remained of the Audit House was the front wall. Apart from Mowat's Fish Market, just out of camera range to the right of the Audit House, everything else around it was also destroyed. (City Heritage Services)

High Street, west side, 1997. The ruins of the Audit House were demolished in the early 1950s, council administration having been moved to the Civic Centre as early as 1932. From 1934 the Audit House was used as the Co-operative Society's meat warehouse until it was destroyed in the blitz. After rebuilding took place in the 1950s, the site was occupied by the Southampton Fruit Exchange but the fruit market industry in Southampton did not expand as rapidly as was anticipated. The site was later taken over by Habitat, the trend-setting furniture, soft furnishing and household goods company.

High Street, *c.* 1954. Although the war had been over for nearly ten years when this photograph was taken, the ruins of the blitzed All Saints' Church were still standing on the corner of the High Street and East Street. Built in 1795 to replace an earlier church, All Saints' Church was completely out of character with the other churches in the vicinity. Its colonnaded façade visually overpowered the surrounding buildings but, despite its imposing appearance, it had a very strong and faithful congregation. The burial ground for the church's dead was further down East Street, roughly where the East Gate car park is today. (Veal Collection)

High Street, 1997. The top of East Street was transformed in 1956 when the ruins of All Saints' Church were demolished to make way for new shops. The buildings still exist in a virtually unchanged state, although the uses to which they have been put have varied over the years. Jordan's shoe shop was the first occupant of the corner site; it was later used by Granada Television Rentals, which occupied the building for many years until just after this photograph was taken. November 1997 saw the building boarded up and empty.

High Street, 1956. The Gaiety Cinema opened for business in 1914 and became the first cinema in Southampton to show 'talkies' in 1929. The photograph shows the old cinema with a 'for sale' sign over the door, while the poster outside advertises H.G. Wells' *War of the Worlds*. Next to the cinema was Misselbrook & Weston's grocery store. It now seems strange that not so very long ago groceries could still be bought in an old-fashioned shop in the High Street. Misselbrook & Weston's company is still thriving, however, with many small supermarkets catering for local needs. (Veal Collection)

High Street, 1997. The cinema and the grocery store were demolished shortly after the top photograph was taken, with the mock-Moorish façade of the Gaiety being replaced by bland 1960s' architecture. The District Bank was on the site of the cinema, while that of the grocery store was occupied by Zurich Assurance. The corner site has seen many different occupants over the years, including a card shop. It is now a place to buy bus tickets with Solent Blue Line. Misselbrook & Weston's site is occupied by an extension to Barclay's Bank.

Houndwell, south side, *c.* 1956. Edwin Jones' department store in Queens Buildings was completely destroyed in the blitz of 1940. A temporary structure was erected on the site of the original store, but it consisted only of a makeshift shop front and display windows, while the main shop was in the basement of the original building. Some of the other departments were moved to temporary locations in Portswood (men's clothing) and Shirley (ladies' and children's clothing). The furniture department continued business in nearby East Street, while the fruit and vegetable shop traded from Hanover Buildings. (Veal Collection)

Houndwell, south side, 1997. Edwin Jones' new building was erected on the site of the original building between 1958 and 1959. Business continued while the rebuilding was going on, but many customers found it confusing because the locations of the various departments changed almost on a daily basis. The building was completed and all the scattered departments were rehoused within it by 1960. The company was taken over by the Debenham Group in the 1970s and continues to trade from the same site.

Houndwell, north side, *c.* 1945. The temporary camp site at Houndwell was the headquarters for the American troops who embarked from Southampton on their way to the Normandy beaches in 1944. The huts remained derelict until the 1950s when they were demolished. Just out of camera range, on the right of the photograph, was the scene of a tragedy in November 1940 when a public air-raid shelter received a direct hit from a German bomb and up to sixty people were killed. The site was ploughed over because so little remained of the victims' bodies, but the Americans weren't allowed to erect their huts on the site. (City Heritage Services)

Houndwell, north side, 1997. Amazingly, the red public telephone box is still intact after fifty years or more. Otherwise the site, opposite Debenham's department store, has reverted to pleasant parkland in the city centre. The mass grave of the wartime bombing victims was marked by the planting of a tree on the fiftieth anniversary of the tragedy in November 1990. A small plaque was erected to the memory of the victims at the same time.

Inner Ring Road, looking north, 1960. The car park behind the old walls looks remarkably deserted in this photograph. Through the gap in the wall is the mound of earth that resulted from the extension of Portland Terrace and, beyond that, work is still continuing on the reconstruction and widening of the road. Most of the buildings that stood in the way of progress have been demolished but a solitary shed – probably part of the old slaughterhouse in Spa Road – remains on the right, behind the modern Bargate Street shops. There are even a few trees in evidence to brighten up the area. (Veal Collection)

Inner Ring Road, looking north, March 1997. Castle Way joins the extended Portland Terrace. The modern Arundel Towers office block, empty and due for demolition in October 1997, dominates the scene but, out of camera view, the row of Regency buildings in Portland Terrace, opposite the junction with Portland Street, has been allowed to survive. The buildings are now listed and used mainly as solicitors' offices.

Inner Ring Road, looking south, 1960. The Inner Ring Road cut a swath through the medieval street plan of Southampton in 1961 to 1963. There was already a gap in the old town wall here, which allowed the new road to go through without too much other destruction. Beyond that many of the ancient streets and lanes were demolished for the sake of this first, radical new scheme to assist the flow of traffic through the city. The mock-Tudor building on the right of the photograph was the Arundel Tower Hotel, erected in 1898 and demolished in 1968. (Veal Collection)

Inner Ring Road, looking south, 1997. In a similar view, the Inner Ring Road now passes though the old city walls. The car parks at either side of the road still exist, but otherwise the aspect is quite different. Castle House flats (opened in 1963) now dominate the skyline, while, since 1990, the ugly and inappropriate footbridge, joining the two halves of the old city wall, still begs the question: 'Whose idea was that, then?'.

Latimer Street, *c.* 1980. The Deanery School, which specialized in preparing young men for a career in the Merchant Marine, stood several hundred yards away from the Deanery Annexe, which was on the corner of Latimer Street and Bernard Street. The annexe, seen in the photograph during its demolition, also provided accommodation for the Southampton Technical College located in nearby St Mary Street; many classes, including the maths class for aspiring Merchant Marine Radio Officers, were held in this building. (Ron Williams)

Latimer Street, 1997. Not long after the demolition of the Deanery Annexe and several other old dilapidated buildings in Latimer Street and nearby Bernard Street, new houses were erected. The presence of the new buildings gave an otherwise run-down area a distinct sense of respectability, which it retains to this day. This photograph shows the rear of some of these buildings that face on to Bernard Street.

Lower Canal Walk, *c.* 1953. In the early twentieth century Lower Canal Walk was a narrow lane that led from Bernard Street to the Town Quay, where, on the corner, the oldest bowling green in the country still exists. There were shops, private dwellings, a couple of pubs and many bait-diggers' premises. The housing, however, was poor and demolition of the area began in the 1930s. The war interrupted the redevelopment, although the bombing did assist in removing many of the remaining old buildings. In the distance you can just make out the outline of the Washington Hotel (now a transport office), while the few trees in the foreground give the scene an almost rural look. (Veal Collection)

Site of Lower Canal Walk, 1997. Fruit and vegetable markets had existed in this area for many years and so, when the area was redeveloped in the late 1950s, the city planners decided that it should be a fruit and vegetable market on a par with London's Covent Garden. The grandiose plans didn't quite work out, but the area still thrives in its chosen specialization. To make the new market area practical and appear symmetrical, the Bernard Street end of Lower Canal Walk was built over; what is left of Lower Canal Walk now leads from Briton Street to the Town Quay.

New Road, looking east, 1954. Much of this area was destroyed in the blitz but, on the left, a car dealer set up in business on the site of the bombed premises, while the Richard Andrews public house was still open for business. Out of the picture, also on the left, is the Southampton Charitable Dispensary, Dental Institute and Humane Society (the dental clinic). On the right of the picture, all that was left after the bombing was the Bay Tree Inn and a motor tyre dealer until no. 34, towards the end of the road, where several private houses and small shops still remained. (Veal Collection)

New Road, looking east, 1997. The scene today is quite different. The left-hand side of the road is now completely taken over by the Southampton Institute. The college was established on the site in 1960 to take over from the old Technical College in St Mary Street and has continually expanded ever since. In the centre, the Clifford House office block was built in the 1960s on the sites of the houses and small shops that escaped the war but couldn't escape redevelopment. Other similar blocks were erected in later years. The Bay Tree Inn on the right, rebuilt in 1955, was renamed the Graduate in 1996.

Orchard Lane, c. 1956. The run-down streets and alleys that were bounded by East Street, Bernard Street and Threefield Lane provided homes for many small shops and businesses. Shown in the photograph are the premises of Frank Blake, the grocer on the corner of College Street, and Ocean Trading (Wholesale) Ltd, which supplied goods to many of the luxury shops on the liners. To the right of the photograph is the entrance to the lounge bar of the Globe Hotel. The Globe Hotel was owned by the Globe Brewery, which was registered by Sir Frederick Perkins & Sons in 1912. The brewery closed in 1925 and Ocean Trading later used the brewery premises in Orchard Lane as its warehouse. (Southampton Archives Services)

Orchard Lane, 1997. The area was cleared in the mid-1950s and replaced by modern council flats, many of which are now privately owned. The Globe Hotel remained intact, although Blake's the grocery shop and Ocean Trading had to go. After redevelopment of the area, the Globe Hotel and the gate that once led into the Ocean Trading warehouse were the only remaining vestiges of the area as it was. The Globe Hotel closed down in 1988 and lay derelict until 1994, when the building was restored and converted to apartments.

Orchard Lane, 1956. For many years Helliwell's greengrocery shop stood on the corner of Orchard Lane and Chandos Street in a very old and run-down part of Southampton, not far from East Street and the fashionable Debenham's department store. The town planning department began to redevelop the area in the late 1930s but was interrupted by the Second World War and the German air-raids. The air-raids were responsible for the destruction of many more of the dilapidated properties in the area but the really big changes came in the late 1950s when the rest of the buildings were demolished. (Southampton Archives Services)

Orchard Lane, 1997. It is no longer possible to take a photograph from exactly the same spot as the earlier photograph. This, however, is about as near as you can get to the corner of Orchard Lane and Chandos Street today. The council flats were first occupied in 1958, mainly by people who had once lived in the old houses in the area. In 1958 the flats were considered to be the height of luxury, many having four bedrooms. However, apart from an electric fire in the living room no heating was provided, so the flats, although spacious, were very cold in the winter months.

Orchard Lane, *c*. 1956. The Diamond Jubilee Inn was one of the few public houses in Southampton that belonged to Lovibond's Greenwich Brewery. In this dilapidated and run-down area, pictured shortly before its demolition, the pub and the neighbouring small businesses, such as Tong's the basket-maker and Rigg's leather stores, were also demolished at the same time. The area was certainly representative of the poorest of housing in Southampton but the demolition of the houses left a void in the community that has never really been refilled. (Southampton Archives Services)

Orchard Lane, 1997. Council flats built in the late 1950s now occupy the sites of many of the run-down buildings that once stood in Orchard Lane and its environs. Although many more people live in the area than in previous years, the community spirit that was prevalent in the years before the Second World War has not been perpetuated. Perhaps people are more comfortable in present times, which is as it should be, but in many ways it is a shame that the old-fashioned communities no longer exist.

Oxford Street, 1956. Once owned by Queen's College in Oxford, the whole of Oxford Street had become dilapidated by the end of the Second World War. The south side of the street is shown in the photograph and, as can be seen, the once elegant early Victorian terraces were in desperate need of attention. Although run down, the buildings provided premises for many local businesses such as travel agents, fruit merchants, tailors and booksellers. There were even two or three private residents in the terrace. (Southampton Archives Services)

Oxford Street, south side, 1997. The whole of the Oxford Street area was restored in the 1980s. The road was blocked off where it met Terminus Terrace so that through traffic was no longer a problem. Where there were once shops that catered for members of the Merchant Navy, new pubs and restaurants opened, and the existing pubs in the area were refurbished to revitalize this part of the city. The terrace of early Victorian houses, having been carefully restored, still provides office accommodation.

Porters Lane, *c.* 1945. Named after the trade of the people who lived in the street many years ago, Porters Lane runs from the High Street to French Street. On the left side is Geddes warehouse, while on the right stands a building known locally as Canute's Palace. There is no real evidence that King Canute actually used the building as a palace: it is Norman and post-dates King Canute by a hundred years or more. However, long before German bombs reduced the building to ruins in 1940, Canute's Palace had fallen into disrepair. The building had been patched up many times over the years, at one time being used both as a warehouse and by a coal merchant. (City Heritage Services)

Porters Lane, 1997. At the end of hostilities in 1945 Canute's Palace was, like much of the lower end of the High Street, in ruins. As the photograph above shows, the ruins were left to themselves for several years. Although Geddes warehouse on the left-hand side was restored and is currently being used as luxury apartments and fine restaurants, the right-hand side of the road was cleaned up and left, like the rest of the area, as a monument to medieval Southampton.

Portland Terrace, looking south, *c.* 1960. The Royal Victoria Assembly Rooms stood in a cul-de-sac in Portland Terrace. When the rooms opened in 1820 they were known simply as the 'New Rooms' and later the 'Archery Rooms'; it wasn't until the visit of Princess Victoria in 1830 that they became known as the 'Royal Victoria Assembly Rooms'. Many social functions were held in these rooms during the nineteenth and early twentieth centuries, but the rooms gradually fell into disuse. Although they survived the blitz of 1940, by 1948 the rooms were being used as offices by the Southampton Gas & Coke Company. (Veal Collection)

Portland Terrace, looking south, March 1997. Regardless of any historical interest, the Assembly Rooms stood in the way of progress in the early 1960s. They were demolished in 1961 to allow the Inner Ring Road to plough its way through Southampton's ancient street plan. The old Coliseum building, which stood on the left of the road, was demolished at the same time. The Arundel Towers office blocks were erected in 1968. They stood empty for six months or more in 1997, awaiting the eventual demolition that began in October of that year.

Portland Terrace, looking north, *c.* 1959. As this photograph shows, Portland Terrace was once an area of very mixed architecture. On the left stood Manchester Street, Everton Street and Clifton Terrace, all of which comprised terraced houses, small corner shops and some pubs. It was a residential area then, and had been for more than 100 years. On the far right, just beyond the tea rooms, was the old Hants & Dorset bus station, while some old Regency buildings are in evidence on the near right. The Civic Centre clock tower can just be seen in the middle distance. (Veal Collection)

Portland Terrace, looking north, 1997. How the scene had changed. On the right, the Regency buildings are still intact and have been renovated several times over the years. Also on the right, the Hants & Dorset bus station was demolished in 1987, the site now being occupied by the Marlands shopping mall. On the left, the small residential streets disappeared in the 1960s, the sites remaining vacant until the multi-storey car park was built in the 1970s and the Asda supermarket was built in the 1980s.

Prospect Place, c. 1945. This unusual little gravelled road ran behind some of the more prominent shops at the northern end of Above Bar Street and, for more than 100 years, housed mainly insurance offices and other business premises rather than retail shops. The part of Prospect Place that faced Above Bar Street, however, housed the premises of the wool store of Fleming, Reid & Company, the Dolcis shoe shop, Samuel's jewellery shop, and H.A. Leon, a company that specialized in fur garments. (Southampton Archives Services)

The site of Prospect Place, 1997. Redevelopment during the late 1950s and early 1960s meant that the quaint Prospect Place had to go. The offices and showrooms of the (then) Southern Gas Board were housed in a brand-new building in the early 1960s and closed down in 1996 when the premises became a pub known as the Old Fat Cat. Part of the original Prospect Place, however, can still be seen at the rear of Tyrrell & Green's department store.

Queensway, 1956. The city planners saw the need for an inner ring road to aid traffic flow in the city when they were planning the rebuilding of Southampton. That rebuilding included the eventual pedestrianization of Above Bar Street, the city's main thoroughfare. This part of the inner ring road was called Queensway (after Edwin Jones' Queens Buildings) and ran across the sites of many of the poor dwellings around East Street and Orchard Lane. Demolition of the area began in the 1930s and was finished in the 1950s. The steel skeleton of Edwin Jones' new department store can be seen rising in the background. (Veal Collection)

Queensway, 1997. Queensway is now one of the busiest roads in the city. It cuts East Street completely in two and has provided new shops and apartments in the old, run-down area between Canal Walk and Orchard Lane. In the forty years since the photograph above was taken, trees have matured along the southern side, shielding the blocks of flats from the inevitable noise that results from a road like Queensway. Edwin Jones' (now Debenham's) building can be seen in the middle distance while the petrol station records early 1997 petrol prices for ever.

Simnel Street, 1971. St Michael's House, a council-run hostel for the homeless, is the main feature of this picture of how Simnel Street used to be. The building was constructed as part of the Housing of the Working Classes Act of 1897, when the area was cleared of slums, and was formally opened in 1899. On the rear ground floor of the building, where Simnel Street sloped away towards the Western Esplanade, were two shops: a confectionery run by John Walker and a general store run by Gertrude Smedley; the building also contained several council apartments for private citizens. (Southampton Archives Services)

Simnel Street, 1997. The council dwellings and St Michael's House were demolished in 1972, the site being vacant for a long time to allow important archaeological excavations to be carried out around the part of the old town walls where Biddlesgate once stood. On redevelopment of the area in 1983, the street was narrowed considerably and closed off permanently to traffic. The one recognizable feature that appears in both photographs is the Queen public house (now called the Atlantic Queen) at the top of the street.

Threefield Lane, *c.* 1956. George Rogers' cycle shop had stood on the corner of Threefield Lane and Chandos Street since before the Second World War. The flat above the shop was let out to various tenants over the years, the one in 1948 being Thomas Sharp, a once common name in Southampton. As the photograph shows, the area fell into disrepair over the years; the building was demolished shortly after the photograph was taken. Next door to the cycle shop at no. 50 was one of the many dilapidated private houses in the street. This one was once occupied by one Charles Lewis, also a common name in the city. (Southampton Archives Services)

Threefield Lane, 1997. Taken from a slightly different angle from the top photograph, this view shows how the corner looked in 1997. Low-rise flats, built in the late 1950s, and trees now occupy the site of the old bicycle shop. On the opposite corner of Chandos Street can be seen the sign of the Anchor and Hope public house. The pub was established in the 1840s and has, remarkably, managed to survive the many changes that have occurred in the area over the years.

Vincents Walk, 1945. Like much of the city centre, this area, behind Above Bar Street, fared badly during the blitz. Most of the buildings remained standing and the Free Trader's Arms public house (the flat-fronted, three-storey building) was still open for business. The ruins of the Above Bar Congregational Church can be seen just beyond that, while in the distance was Hendy's Garage which had, until just before this photograph was taken, still been assembling Spitfire fighter planes after the Supermarine Works in Woolston were destroyed. All buildings were demolished in 1952 for redevelopment of the area. (Southampton Archives Services)

Vincents Walk, 1997. Despite much research, I cannot discover the person after whom this street was named. In 1997, however, it is still an important street as far as the city is concerned because it houses the major local bus terminals. As far as the street itself goes, the Fur Stores once stood on the corner of Hanover Buildings and Vincents Walk. That building was bombed and Perrin's furniture store was later erected on the site; Perrin's shop was later acquired by Dillons the bookshop. Marks & Spencer now occupies the site of the Above Bar Congregational Church, while Hendy's Garage is now part of Woolworths.

Westgate Street, *c.* 1970. The view down Westgate Street from Bugle Street shows that much of the area was bombed during the blitz. Some old cottages remained in Cuckoo Lane but they weren't historically significant. The area was cleared completely in the late 1960s, modernistic houses in Scandinavian style being erected on the northern side of the street. The area on the southern side of the street became a temporary car park until plans were finalized for redevelopment. In the distance is the Tudor Merchants' Hall, covered in scaffolding and tarpaulin as extensive renovations take place after many years of neglect. (City Heritage Services)

Westgate Street, 1997. Westgate, through which the Pilgrim Fathers passed to board the *Mayflower* in 1620, is now restored completely, as is the Tudor Merchants' Hall. A pleasant square occupies the site of the temporary car park seen in the photograph above. To the left of the street, modern housing in keeping with the overall historic aspect of the area was erected in the 1980s. Cuckoo Lane was included in the redevelopment of this area and newly married couples from the nearby Register Office often use it as a photographic backdrop.

Windsor Terrace, *c.* 1950. Plested's pie shop has been an institution among Sotonians from the 1930s until the present day. Situated behind the Grand Theatre and opposite the bus station, the original location could not have been better for one of the first 'takeaways' in the city. The pies were freshly cooked on the premises and simply oozed lovely meaty gravy – not the easiest of things to eat after an evening at the theatre, but delicious just the same! To buy your pie, you entered the small door to the right of the building and were served at a hatchway along the corridor. Often the queue stretched out into the street. (Veal Collection)

Windsor Terrace, 1997. Plested's original pie shop was pulled down in 1960 when the Grand Theatre was demolished and much of the area redeveloped. Plested's shop found itself in new premises on the corner of Manchester Street and Windsor Terrace, from where it traded until 1987 when the area was again redeveloped to make way for the Marlands shopping complex. Plested's pie shop now trades from premises in both East Street and Shirley High Street.

York Buildings, *c.* 1945. German bombs destroyed much of East Street and the streets that adjoined it. York Buildings at the top of East Street was among the worst hit. The old-fashioned shops that traded from the street disappeared for ever and the scene was one of desolation for several years. The bombing also severely damaged Cooper's Brewery, which had brewed beer from York Buildings since the end of the eighteenth century. The tall brewery chimney was spared in the bombing and can be seen on the right. (Veal Collection)

York Buildings, 1997. The war damage in the area was cleared up in the 1950s and new shops and offices were erected; Montague Burton's tailor's shop was the first to occupy the corner premises. Cooper's Brewery was patched up and taken into the Watney Group in 1943. Brewing ceased in the 1950s and the building became a bottling plant. After Watney pulled out, the building was used as a warehouse before being demolished in the early 1990s to make way for the Bargate Centre.

DOWN BY THE DOCKS

*TOWN QUAY, THE DOCKS, WESTERN
ESPLANADE AND THE FLOATING BRIDGE*

Central Baths, Western Esplanade, 1961. Photographed shortly after they opened, the Central Swimming Baths were built to replace the old Lido and swimming baths that stood further west along the Western Esplanade. In their heyday the baths attracted many Sotonians and, with the Olympic-size swimming pool, they were the local training centre for many international swimming competitions, including the Olympic Games. In a bid to attract more customers after business began to tail off, the baths were renamed Centre 2000 in the 1980s and a massive water chute was erected on the back of the building. (Southampton Archives Services)

Centre 2000, Western Esplanade, 1997. After the baths closed in the early 1990s, the building was boarded up and allowed to fall into disrepair. The building was later used by squatters and gypsies and became a blot on the landscape, especially when compared to the five-star Grand Harbour Hotel that stood next door. After much procrastination by the city planners the decision was made to demolish the old swimming baths and erect new, state-of-the-art swimming baths and leisure facilities on the site ready for the year 2000. The photograph shows the sad old building being demolished in March 1997.

Floating Bridge, c. 1962. There had been a ferry across the River Itchen from Southampton to Woolston for many, many years before the chain-driven Floating Bridge was inaugurated in November 1836. The Floating Bridge remained in service until 1976, being refurbished and replaced many times over the years. The photograph also shows an early hovercraft on its way to the Isle of Wight from the hoverport on the Woolston side of the river. In the distance, on the left, can be seen the old Vickers Supermarine works where the Spitfire fighter plane was developed. The building was badly damaged during the blitz of 1940 but was partially restored in the 1960s to serve as offices. (Southampton Archives Services)

Site of the Floating Bridge Hard, 1997. From a similar viewpoint, the scene is entirely different. The Floating Bridge Hard still exists, now being used by the Southampton Sailing School to train young people in the art of sailing. The biggest difference between the photographs is the towering Itchen Bridge. This opened in 1977 and, in effect, brought the eastern side of the River Itchen closer to the centre of Southampton.

The Lido, Western Esplanade, 1973. One of the most popular of Southampton's attractions, the Lido was used by many Sotonians over several decades. The Lido was on land that was reclaimed from the River Test in the 1930s and indoor swimming baths were also connected to the outdoor Lido. The photograph, taken in about 1973, shows the site of the demolished indoor swimming baths in the foreground. The Lido, in the centre of the picture, remained as popular as ever. The Lido was later closed and allowed to decay, while wild plants and other wildlife settled on the site. The ubiquitous buddleia was a prime feature on the site and marine life flourished in the old swimming pool. (Veal Collection)

Site of the Lido, 1997. The site of the Lido was cleared for redevelopment in the 1980s. An Asda supermarket was erected on the sites of the old residential streets that were once in the area. Space was needed for people to park their cars while they went shopping, so the Lido was given over to a car park. The view in both photographs is from the National Car Parks site in Portland Terrace. Above, the view is of a pleasant scene of people enjoying themselves around a swimming pool, while the bottom photograph shows merely the view from one multi-storey car park to another.

Mayflower Park, *c*. 1968. Located in a small area of reclaimed land between the Royal Pier and the Western Docks, Mayflower Park was neglected until the 1960s. During the war years, and until well into the 1950s, the reclaimed land was occupied by concrete tank traps and was not a very pleasant place to visit. However, in the 1960s plans went ahead to make the area into a pleasant one for citizens to use as an amenity centre. A car park was laid out on the side facing the river, so that people could view the passing shipping from the comfort of their cars, and the open space was transformed into a playground for children. (Southampton Archives Services)

Mayflower Park, 1997. The park in 1997 is well established. The temporary concrete tubes that were once used as children's playthings have been replaced by permanent adventure playgrounds and the whole area has been landscaped. A solitary crane rising in the background serves as a reminder of how close the park is to the docks. Once a year the park is taken over by the enormously successful International Boat Show. September 1997 saw the twenty-ninth such show and over 150,000 people are reported to have attended.

Terminus station, *c.* 1945. A Standard Flying Twelve motor car, still with its wings outlined in wartime white, stands outside what was once the most important railway station in Southampton. The station opened in about 1840 and for years served the many passengers that passed through the port on their way to foreign parts via the many sea-going liners that sailed from Southampton. The magnificent South Western Hotel was adjacent to the railway station, so everyone's needs were catered for in one way or another. (Southampton Archives Services)

Terminus station, 1997. In the late 1960s, when the sea-going passenger trade began to tail off, the Terminus station no longer had a useful function and closed down in 1966. The building was neglected for many years and many people thought that it should be demolished. An enterprising gambling company, however, decided differently and transformed the old railway station into a casino, thus adding to the attractions in this revitalized part of the city.

The Town Quay, 1985. Standing on the corner of the High Street and Town Quay, the original Sun Hotel was completely destroyed during the war. The pub was rebuilt in 1944 as a 'temporary' structure on the foundations of the original eighteenth-century hotel and remained there until 1990, serving as a reminder of the deprivations that Sotonians had suffered in the war years. St Julian's Chapel is to the left in the background of the photograph. The chapel was used by French Huguenot refugees in the sixteenth century and to this day it is known as the 'French Church'. (Gallaher Collection)

Town Quay, 1997. The Sun Hotel closed down in June 1990 and remained boarded up and derelict until 1994 when the building was demolished. After important archaeological excavations, the Notobene House office block was erected on the site. So far none of the office suites has been occupied and the new building remains empty. The Harland & Wolfe sheds have since gone from the right of the background but new office blocks have appeared.

Western Docks, 1956. An unusual sight in Southampton was that of HM Submarine *Sea Scout*, a Royal Navy S-Class submarine, coming alongside Berth 101 in the Western Docks on 16 March 1956. The submarine was on a courtesy call to Southampton and was open to the public while she was in dock. The three other small vessels already alongside Berth 101, including the one billowing black smoke, were probably on courtesy calls too. A row of Union Castle liners can be seen in the background – a common sight in the 1950s when the Union Castle Line ran its regular service from Southampton to South Africa. (Southampton Archives Services)

Western Docks, September 1997. Despite the existence of the container berth at the far western end of the Western Docks, some ships still use the original berths of the Western Docks. The photograph shows a Geest container ship with a cargo of bananas about to be unloaded. In the far distance can be seen the P&O cruise liner *Canberra*, affectionately known as 'The Great White Whale' after service in the Falkland Islands conflict. The liner had arrived in Southampton after her final cruise the day before this photograph was taken. Sotonians will always have fond memories of such a lovely ship.

Western Esplanade, 1971. The city walls were much neglected in the latter part of the nineteenth century and fell into disrepair. The Housing of the Working Classes Act of 1897 resulted in the demolition of this part of the crumbling city walls and the construction of model artisans' dwellings, aimed at replacing the slums that existed in the area with good housing for working people. In 1944 American troops lined up alongside the houses while they awaited embarkation to the Normandy beaches for the D-Day invasion. Many of them carved their names and home addresses into the walls of the houses before they left England to fight the Germans in France, but how many were to return? No one knows. (Southampton Archives Services)

Western Esplanade, 1997. The artisans' dwellings were demolished in the 1970s to make way for new improved housing. The area looks much tidier now, but no one knows what happened to the wall that contained the inscriptions of the American troops. A similar wall, on the opposite side of the road, had a few inscriptions and some of the bricks are held by Southampton City Heritage Services, but the main wall seems to have gone for ever, taking much of the city's recent history with it.

Western Esplanade, *c.* 1960. The view across the reclaimed land was not too inspiring in 1960 because the full potential of the land had not yet been realized. The chimney of Pirelli's cable factory, which can be seen beyond the public mortuary building, dominates the skyline. The chimneys of the Southern Electricity power station, where Toys R Us stands today, take second place because they are that much further away. (Veal Collection)

Western Esplanade, 1997. In this view you can see how the Western Esplanade has changed in the last thirty years. The old mortuary building disappeared many years ago and the five-star Grand Harbour Hotel now dominates the scene. The road itself has been narrowed and now includes artists' impressions of how the road may have looked in medieval times when the water came right up to the old walls. Impressions of tides and old-fashioned boats are laid out in the new paved area.

Western Esplanade, *c.* 1965. The new public swimming baths had been erected just a year or two before this photograph was taken. The arcades of the old city walls and the solitary horse trough, dedicated to the memory of Madame Maes, whose house once stood on the site, can be seen in the foreground of the photograph. Traffic was lighter in those days, so the young man on his bicycle is probably not as brave as he looks. (City Heritage Services)

Western Esplanade, 1997. The scene here is much busier than in the earlier photograph. It would take a brave person to cycle around the area today. The right-hand side of the road still looks much the same as it has done for many years; even Madame Maes' horse trough is still intact. The left-hand side of this busy road, however, is now dominated by the Grand Harbour Hotel, which was opened to the public in 1993.

West Quay Road, 1953. The photograph shows how the junction of West Quay Road and the Western Esplanade looked over forty years ago. The land was reclaimed from a natural bay in the river during the 1930s. The Western Docks (then known as the New Docks) and Rank's Flour Mill, both of which can be seen in the distance, were the first buildings to be constructed on the reclaimed land, but the outbreak of the Second World War in 1939 prevented any further development of the land and the area remained neglected for many years. (Veal Collection)

West Quay Road, 1997. The commercial development of West Quay Road began in earnest in 1965 with the construction of the Skyways Hotel (now called the Post House Hotel). The Pirelli General cable factory had long dominated the area; an overhead gantry and some large cable drums can still be seen on the right-hand side of the road. The other major development, apart from the large number of businesses and commercial premises that now line the road, was the construction of the Odeon Leisure Centre in 1997. The area, away from the town centre, is now devoted to industrial, shopping and leisure facilities.

TO THE EAST

NORTHAM, ST MARYS, KINGSLAND AND CHAPEL

Bellevue Terrace, *c.* 1967. Bellevue Terrace once formed one leg of a busy five-road junction, the other roads being Onslow Road, St Marys Road, Dorset Street and Bellevue Road. Running from St Marys Road to the Inner Avenue, Bellevue Terrace was transformed into a cul-de-sac during the 1960s when the Inner Ring Road swept through Dorset Street and cut off access from Bellevue Road to Onslow Road and St Marys Road. The photograph shows how the area looked just after the road was turned into a cul-de-sac. Parking was allowed anywhere, or so it seems. The antique shop later became an 'ethnic furniture' shop which for many years sold bamboo goods. (Southampton Archives Services)

Bellevue Terrace, 1997. Superficially, Bellevue Terrace has changed very little in the thirty years between the two photographs. The shrubs at the end of the road are mature trees in 1997 while the former antiques shop is now derelict. Although the apparent condition of the houses in Bellevue Terrace looks significantly better than in the 1967 photograph, the buildings are now used mainly for rented apartment accommodation. The whole area around Onslow Road is now quite run down but there are plans for improvement. Parking is now for residents only!

Chapel Road, *c.* 1963. Chapel Road and the surrounding streets once comprised a thriving community of shops, pubs, businesses and private houses. The area had become very dilapidated by the beginning of the 1960s and the whole lot was eventually demolished. The photograph, taken in about 1963, shows Finn the greengrocer's shop boarded up, waiting for the inevitable bulldozer to come along. On the corner of Nelson Street, however, Ernest Chard's butcher's shop is still open for business and Spagagna's boot repair shop on the other corner is still thriving. (Southampton Archives Services)

Chapel Road, 1997. This shows how the area has changed dramatically in the last thirty years. The road is devoted to industrial units in 1997, while Southampton Technical College has acquired much of the area on the right-hand side of the road. Trees now hide the ugly sight of a haulier's premises where the little shops once stood.

Dorset Street, c. 1965. The area here was little affected by the bombing of 1940, but the housing was not of the best quality. Narrow Northam Street and Bellevue Street, with their old and dilapidated dwellings, led from Dorset Street to St Marys Road, while Dorset Street itself joined up with St Marys Road, Bellevue Road, Bellevue Terrace and East Park Terrace. In the distance on the left is St Matthew's Mission Hall, on the corner of Bellevue Street, while on the corner of Northam Street stood Park House. Further up the road on the right stood the Gladstone Club, which was relocated when the area was redeveloped. (Southampton Archives Services)

Dorset Street, 1997. The offices of British Gas dominate the scene today. The little, old-fashioned streets that were once part of the area were demolished in the late 1960s when the Inner Ring Road was constructed. The British Gas offices were built some time later, opening in 1977 when the company moved its administrative headquarters from Winchester Road to this purpose-built site in the centre of the city. The Charlotte Place traffic scheme and car park were developed at the same time.

East Park Terrace, *c*. 1965. The photograph shows the corner of East Park Terrace and Compton Walk. Although the area was not damaged by German bombs during the war, the city council had other plans for this run-down part of the city. Most of the houses in East Park Terrace and Compton Walk had early Victorian origins and were in serious need of repair and refurbishment. Southampton, however, had a serious traffic problem and, in an attempt to solve part of the problem, the junction of East Park Terrace and Compton Walk disappeared to become the Charlotte Place traffic system. (Southampton Archives Services)

East Park Terrace, 1997. If the junction of East Park Terrace and Compton Walk was still in existence, this would be the view looking towards the east. A fragment of Compton Walk does still exist, but it leads only from St Marys Road to Charlotte Place car park in the centre of the traffic roundabout. Otherwise the whole area has changed beyond recognition.

Kingsland Square, *c.* 1955. The Kingsland Picture Theatre opened on a site adjacent to Kingsland Square in 1914. The cinema was an immediate success and attracted many people from those who visited the Kingsland Market. However, the building was destroyed by enemy action in 1940 and the ruins remained derelict until 1955 when the site was cleared to provide the space to expand the market. There had been a market on Kingsland Square for years but, after 1955, it expanded beyond recognition. In the background of the photograph can be seen Maxwell's, the tailors. Anyone who was a teenager in the 1950s will remember this shop and that of Sydney Man's Shop, also in St Mary Street. (Veal Collection)

Kingsland Square, 1997. Instead of the market being held just once or twice weekly, Kingsland Square became a permanent market-place in the 1970s when traders rented regular sites from the agent. In later years the market was roofed over and it is now a prominent daily feature in the lives of the many people who still live in the area. Many of the market stalls belong to people of Asian origin and so this is the place to find exotic herbs and spices for that special Eastern meal.

Millbank Street, *c.* 1958. Millbank Street is a continuation of Princes Street, leading on down to Marine Parade and Albert Road. At one time the area was densely occupied by old houses of the poorest quality, as can be seen here. Although the wartime bombing of Northam left much damage, the remainder of the area was cleared of the bad housing in the late 1950s and early 1960s. Modern new flats were erected on the sites of the old houses. The old street pattern went for ever but one or two bits of the old streets, such as York Street, William Street and Kent Street, can still be seen here and there. (Southampton Archives Services)

Millbank Street, 1997. The years between the demolition of the old-fashioned houses and the construction of the modern flats also saw the planting of trees to enhance the appearance of the area and (eventually) to hide the flats from the road, as well as helping to reduce the level of noise pollution from such a busy road. The trees are now mature, so it is hard to believe that the two photographs are actually of the same site. Apart from the flats, most of this area has been given over to industry. Industrial units of many different kinds dominate the area in 1997.

Northam Road, 1949. The first bridge at Northam was a wooden structure, built in 1797. That bridge was replaced by an iron bridge in 1889, which in turn was replaced by the present-day bridge that opened in October 1954. The photograph shows the road as it was before construction of today's bridge, which was one of the first in the country to be made from pre-stressed concrete. The Plaza Cinema can just be seen on the left of the picture; the gigantic concrete slabs that went to make up the new bridge were made in the children's recreation ground that was once in Radcliffe Road, behind the cinema. (City Heritage Services)

Northam Road, 1997. The Plaza Cinema closed down in November 1957, the premises being taken over by Southern Television; much of the surrounding area was demolished at about the same time. The Plaza building has since been expanded and altered until nothing of the original remains. TVS later took over from Southern Television and now the franchise is operated by Meridian. Northam Bridge is still on the main thoroughfare out to the east of the city, but the construction of the Itchen Bridge and the M27 has eased the traffic congestion for many people from both sides of the river.

Northam Road, *c.* 1958. Frederick Snell's restaurant was a favourite eating place in the area between Belvidere Terrace and Cable Street. The restaurant stood right next door to the old Engineer's Arms public house and was therefore popular among the drinking public. George Beuzeval's tobacconist shop was on the other side of the restaurant, while other businesses in this part of Northam Road included the Mayfair Confectionery Store, the Southern Co-operative Laundry and Alfred Corbyn the butcher. (Southampton Archives Services)

Northam Road, 1997. The side of Northam Road between Belvidere Terrace and Princes Street was completely demolished in the late 1950s. The Prince of Wales public house on the corner of Princes Street was allowed to remain, while at the other end the Engineer's Arms also survived demolition. The part of the road where Snell's restaurant once stood was never redeveloped and advertising placards have occupied the site for years.

Northam Road, *c.* 1958. The Northam Garage was one of the largest single businesses in this particular part of Northam Road. Located on the corner of Northam Road and York Street, the garage premises stretched over two separate addresses and incorporated the adjoining house as office accommodation. The solitary petrol pump outside the garage indicates that it was a working garage and not a filling station. Just to the left of the photograph can be seen part of the Wonder Inn public house, which was named after an old paddle steamer that plied between Southampton and the Channel Islands in the 1850s. (Southampton Archives Services)

Northam Road, 1997. Most of the area was demolished in the late 1950s and replaced by modern flats and shops. The tradition of old-fashioned shops in Northam Road did not die immediately, however. Standing at right angles to Northam Road, on the left of the photograph, there was everything to sustain life in the twentieth century, including a butcher, a grocer, a greengrocer, a baker and a newsagent. To make the scene complete there was also a hairdresser, an ironmonger's shop, a chemist and an off-licence. The shops still exist but pleasant trees now dominate the area.

St Andrews Road, *c*. 1965. Named after the nearby St Andrew's Presbyterian Church (the 'Scottish Church'), St Andrews Road led from the Six Dials to East Park Terrace. The south-west side of the road was destroyed during the blitz and the area was used as allotments for many years. The north-east side, however, as seen in the photograph, remained more or less intact until the area was redeveloped in the late 1960s and early 1970s when the Charlotte Place and Six Dials traffic schemes came into being. (Southampton Archives Services)

St Andrews Road, 1997. The Charlotte Place traffic scheme diverted the top part of St Andrews Road around the back of the buildings seen in the photograph above. The old buildings were demolished and that part of St Andrews Road became a cul-de-sac. New houses, erected in the early 1970s, are seen in the equivalent scene today. The road now forms a pleasant oasis in an otherwise busy part of the city.

St Marys Road, *c.* 1972. Superficially, St Marys Road has changed little in the last twenty-five years but the occupants of the building have been many and varied. The building next door to the Newtown Inn on the left was an Italian restaurant and take-away in 1972 and next to that was the San Toy tobacconist's and confectionery shop, which had stood on that site for many years. Then there was the Freetone Hi-Fi shop, followed by International Cleaners. The remainder of the shops down to Newtown Fabrics on the corner of Brintons Terrace had various other occupants and the area had a feeling of variety and permanence. (Southampton Archives Services)

St Marys Road, 1997. The shops have seen many different occupants over the years. The Newtown Inn was renamed the Oliver Goldsmith in 1993. The Etna Restaurant is now a Greek take-away. The long-established tobacconist's shop later sold exotic fish, while the hi-fi shop is now a sex shop! The rest of the shops in the row have been combined and converted into a night club. Far from the feeling of permanence that the street once had, there is now an atmosphere of decay, as witnessed by the bags of rubbish left in the street.

St Marys Road, *c.* 1975. Major development of the area can be seen. The little streets that led off from St Marys Road have gone, but the old Southampton Co-operative Society's large department store can still be seen, although boarded up and disused. The many shops, pubs and other businesses that lined the western side of St Marys Road fell victim to the bulldozer just before the photograph was taken. The (then) new right turn into Charlotte Place is sign-posted to the City Centre and the West. The fenced-off site was later to become the administrative headquarters of British Gas. (Southampton Archives Services)

St Marys Road, 1997. Apart from the building on the corner of Brintons Terrace, which is now a furniture shop, the area looks quite different here. The new British Gas offices on the right opened in 1977, but the old Southampton Co-operative Society building remained boarded up and derelict for many years. The building, on the corner of Compton Walk, was finally demolished in the 1980s but the site is still unused.

St Marys Road, *c.* 1950. The Six Dials end of St Marys Road seems to have been popular with both new and second-hand furniture stores. There were at least three within a few doors of each other in the 1950s, but the most famous was the SPQR store that had premises in the old Connaught Hall. The letters had no grandiose Roman meaning like '*Senatus Populesque Romanus*', they simply stood for 'Small Profits, Quick Returns'! The shop specialized in selling furniture that had been discarded by shipping companies when liners were refitted. There was nothing wrong with the furniture, indeed it was usually of high quality, but it was at a price people could afford to pay. (Graham Cave Collection)

St Marys Road, 1997. The SPQR furniture shop was demolished in the late 1960s. That was when Clifford House was built in New Road and east-bound traffic around the Six Dials was diverted from New Road, through Brintons Road, and back into Northam Road. For several years the site was occupied by a public car park but, when the present Six Dials traffic scheme came into existence, the area was cleared, modern houses were erected and trees were planted. It is impossible to accurately identify the site of the SPQR shop today but the photograph shows roughly where it once stood.

St Mary Street, *c.* 1960. The building on the corner of St Mary Street and James Street saw many, many uses over the years. This photograph shows it as the Band Box, a musical instrument shop. Over the years, however, it had been used as a nightclub (The Ace of Clubs) and a jazz club (*Le Rat Morte*). The building was demolished in the early 1970s when the rest of this particular area was redeveloped. The Oddfellows' Hall, to the left of the building, continued to be used until it was decommissioned in the 1970s and lay derelict for several years. (Southampton Archives Services)

St Mary Street, 1997. How different the scene looks in 1997. The Band Box has long since disappeared and, rather than put the land to good use, an advertising placard now occupies the site. Oddfellows' Hall was refurbished in the 1980s to become private apartments. The name of the building is now simply 'one-thirty-five St Mary Street'. The pointed façade of the building was removed at the same time. James Street now exists in name only and modern buildings, including a church, have been erected on the sites of the old houses.

Six Dials, c. 1965. The junctions of New Road, St Andrews Road, St Marys Road, St Marks Road, Northam Road and St Mary Street were known collectively as the Six Dials. Even when traffic was light, the Six Dials caused major hold-ups. One attempt to alleviate the problem came in the late 1940s when a roundabout was constructed in the centre of the Six Dials. Tramcars, however, could not negotiate the roundabout, so the tracks went right through it. A later system, after the last tramcar had gone, is seen in the photograph above. Northam Road was made into a one-way street west-bound, while east-bound traffic was diverted through Brintons Road and then on to Northam Road. (Southampton Archives Services)

Site of Six Dials, 1997. After many years of traffic being diverted through the one-way system, the city planners decided to demolish everything in sight and run a brand-new road parallel with the western end of Northam Road. The result was that, although the traffic runs a lot easier now and pedestrians are helped by the myriad of underpasses in the area, that part of the old Northam Road has been reduced to a cul-de-sac and the Six Dials has disappeared in everything but name.

South Front, c. 1965. South Front bounded the Kingsland area of the city on the southern side. Kingsland itself was an early target for the city planners in the 1930s and most of the area had been demolished by the time war broke out in 1939. South Front, however, survived both the demolition of the 1930s and the blitz. The road originally ran from Palmerston Road to St Mary Street but Kingsway cut it short when St Mary Street was bypassed in the late 1960s. As can be seen from the photograph, the buildings were an interesting mixture of shops, houses, pubs and various office premises. (Southampton Archives Services)

South Front, 1997. The untidy but interesting mixture of various styles of architecture in South Front was swept away in the 1970s. Tidy apartment buildings were erected on the sites of the old buildings: the archway in the modern buildings marks the spot where Broad Green once was. The sole remaining original building can still be seen. It was the Robert Burns public house (the white building in the distance), which was demolished just a few weeks after the photograph was taken. The site of the pub is now part of Hendy's Garage.

Union Road, Northam, *c.* 1950. The photograph shows the view from Princes Street, across Northam Road, into Summer Street and on to Radcliffe Road. On the left of the foreground is the Prince of Wales public house, while on the right of the foreground are the premises of Marine Shops Suppliers, the ships' chandler. The vacant plot on the right-hand side of the road is all that remains of the houses that were bombed in 1940. In the far distance can be seen a row of terraced houses that used to exist in Radcliffe Road. (City Heritage Services)

Union Road, Northam, 1997. The Prince of Wales public house still remains, as do most of the houses in Summer Street. This part of Northam Road is now a very busy junction, controlled by the inevitable set of traffic lights. In the far distance, Radcliffe Road still exists but the row of terraced houses has long since gone, and part of the area is now occupied by a Hindu temple. The bomb site on the right-hand side is now a car park, surrounded by trees.

TO THE NORTH

LONDON ROAD, BEDFORD PLACE, PORTSWOOD, SWAYTHLING AND BURGESS ROAD

Amoy Street, *c.* 1965. Delightful Bedford Place still maintains a certain village atmosphere near the centre of the city. Not too long ago, however, many of the side streets leading from Bedford Place were also pleasant to behold. Amoy Street was such a street. Although old, the rows of terraced buildings here provided homes for many Southampton people. With the New Forest Stag public house on the corner of Henry Street and Amoy Street and the shops in Bedford Place, everyone's needs were catered for. (Southampton Archives Services)

Amoy Street, 1997. In the name of progress, the old houses in Amoy Street were demolished in the early 1970s. The buildings were pretty to look at but they dated back to the 1850s and were in a state of bad repair. New houses were erected on the left-hand side of the road, while the right-hand side of the road became a municipal car park. The pub on the corner of Henry Street was never replaced but the new houses are still close enough to Bedford Place to enjoy all of its other amenities.

Banister Street, *c*. 1958. Banister Street (sometimes spelt Bannister Street) was divided into two parts: Upper Banister Street and Lower Banister Street. The street derives its name from the family that owned the land in years gone by: the Banasatre family had owned land in the area since the fifteenth century. The old houses, however, did not bring much credit on the family. They were small, early Victorian back-to-back dwellings with a shared toilet and no facilities for taking a bath. In spite of that, they remained occupied until the early 1970s when the area was redeveloped. (Southampton Archives Services)

Banister Street, 1997. The whole area looks different in the 1990s. The old, tumble-down dwellings of Upper and Lower Banister Street were demolished in the 1970s to allow vehicular access to the shops in Bedford Place. Although some new additions were built on to the shops in Bedford Place, the bulk of the redevelopment in Upper Banister Street meant sacrificing old buildings for the sake of a car park and delivery area. Lower Banister Street fared worse for none of its old buildings survived.

Bevois Valley Road, *c.* 1958. Sir Bevois was a legendary knight from the fourteenth century. His name had been associated with this area since the sixteenth century and the name was later applied to high-class residences in the area, such as Bevois Mount. The district began to be developed from pleasant fields and orchards to housing in the middle of the nineteenth century and Bevois Valley Road was the major thoroughfare. From Ancasta Road, going north to Forster Road, stood a long terrace of small houses, distinguished by the niches in the walls, each of which housed a small statue. Many shops and small businesses, such as Charles Lanham, the furnisher, had traded here for a number of years. (Southampton Archives Services)

Bevois Valley Road, 1997. Redevelopment of the western side of Bevois Valley Road began in the late 1950s when the Mount Hotel on the corner of Ancasta Road was taken over by a used-car dealer. However nice the terrace of houses looked, they were not in very good condition and had cramped accommodation, and so they were the next to go during the 1960s. That side of Bevois Valley Road was never redeveloped and is now dominated completely by used-car dealers. Just out of camera shot, on the right of the photograph, is Thomas Lewis Way, which now takes traffic around the bottlenecks of Portswood and Swaythling.

Burgess Road and Hill Lane Junction, *c.* 1960. As this part of the city evolved in the early part of the twentieth century, going east along Winchester Road brought you to a dangerous 'Y' junction where Burgess Road joined Winchester Road. To make matters worse, regardless of which direction you took, Hill Lane crossed both roads just a few yards later. The photograph shows the view from Hill Lane, across Burgess Road and on to Winchester Road. Various methods were used to make the flow of traffic easier, including 'Halt' signs but, as this part of the city continued to expand, the city planners had to take more drastic action. (City Heritage Services)

Burgess Road and Hill Lane Junction, 1997. As can be seen from the top photograph, Burgess Road was once the main road. All that was changed in the 1960s when a large roundabout was constructed at the junction of Winchester Road and Hill Lane. Part of Burgess Road, behind the petrol station became a cul-de-sac. The scheme helped with the traffic flow but, as traffic increased over the years, other developments, such as the mini-roundabout at the junction of Hill Lane and Burgess Road, were introduced.

Burton Road, *c.* 1970. Burton Road is a little-known cul-de-sac that leads from Milton Road, not far from the Dell football ground, in the Fitzhugh area of the city. A footpath once led from Burton Road to Archers Road, past St Mark's Church, St Mark's Parish Hall and St Mark's Church of England School, all of which can be seen in the middle distance. All the buildings of St Mark were late Victorian and faced out on to Archers Road. Seen here is the rear of the buildings, with the church on the right. (Veal Collection)

Burton Road, 1997. St Mark's Church and most of the associated buildings were demolished in 1983; St Mark's Hall, however, was modernized and partially rebuilt on its original site. The land was used to build three-storeyed town houses in this popular area of the city. St Mark's School transferred to the premises of Western Secondary School in Stafford Road in 1968 and the building in Burton Road was then used as a storehouse. This photograph shows the street looking much the same as it did in the 1970s, although the tall chimneys on the buildings on the right have disappeared.

Carlton Place, *c.* 1960. Another of the quaint streets that lead off Bedford Place, Carlton Place was largely altered in the 1970s when the area between Bedford Place and London Road was redeveloped. The area was badly bombed during the war, especially the London Road side of the street, on the right of the photograph. However, the road did provide accommodation for a wide variety of trades. For instance, in 1962 no. 30 was the office of the 'Territorial & Auxiliary Forces of Hampshire and the Isle of Wight' and no. 28 was Noyce's general dealer's shop. Many other different companies used this street – and there was even room for the odd private house or two. (Southampton Archives Services)

Carlton Place, 1997. Despite the presence of the modern buildings at the Bedford Place end of the street, which replaced Noyce's shop, Carlton Place looks very much the same as it did so many years ago. Its two public houses, the Pensioner's Arms and the Cricketer's Arms, are still intact although very much altered over the years. On the whole, however, the street still maintains its old-fashioned village look, in keeping with Bedford Place, in spite of a large, modern and incongruous college bookshop occupying the Carlton Crescent end of the road.

Cumberland Place, *c.* 1945. This grand terrace of Regency houses was erected when Southampton was a major spa town. At that time the area around the Polygon was being developed with splendid town houses for the many better-off people who came to Southampton to 'take the waters'. After the town was no longer fashionable, the buildings were gradually taken over for office use, mainly by surveyors, solicitors, accountants and insurance companies. The southern end of the terrace was destroyed during the wartime bombing of the city and lay in ruins for several years. (Southampton Archives Services)

Cumberland Place, 1997. The bombed buildings at the southern end of Cumberland Place were removed and replaced by the modern Queens Keep in the late 1960s. The frontages of the rest of the old Regency terrace have been allowed to remain more or less intact, although they have all been renovated and smartened up over the years. As in previous years, the houses are still used as office accommodation, although insurance companies seem to predominate in the 1990s.

General Hospital, *c.* 1980. Although the address of the General Hospital is Tremona Road, Shirley, you have to travel more or less north to get to it. Work began on the Shirley Warren Poor Law Infirmary in 1900 on the north-west edge of the town and the hospital opened formally in 1902. A nurses' home was also added in 1902. The hospital became known as the Borough Hospital in 1929 and saw many changes over the years, including the addition of a maternity wing in 1938. However, its outward appearance still remained much the same as when it first opened in 1902. The name changed to the General Hospital in 1948 with the advent of the National Health Service. (City Heritage Services)

General Hospital, 1997. Starting with the addition of a neurological unit in 1966, in the last four decades the hospital has been subjected to much alteration and expansion. The new main entrance was opened in 1977 and includes several shops and a café. The maternity unit was demolished in 1981 and a brand-new maternity hospital, known as the Princess Anne Hospital, was built in nearby Coxford Road. More recent developments included the transfer of the Eye Hospital from Bedford Place to new, purpose-built premises in the grounds of the General Hospital in 1994.

London Road, looking south, *c*. 1951. London Road was very badly hit in the blitz of 1940; the western side of this once elegant road of Victorian shops and houses was completely destroyed. The eastern side fared slightly better but it lost not only St Paul's Church but also the Unitarian Church, which had stood on the corner of London Road and Bellevue Road. Lloyds Bank managed to continue doing business, albeit in a patched-up, temporary building, but many other long-standing firms in London Road had to move elsewhere and continue their businesses in temporary locations. (Veal Collection)

London Road, looking south, 1997. After it was rebuilt in the early 1960s, London Road welcomed back many of its previous businesses. During the blitz David Greig had continued to trade in one of his many grocery shops on the eastern side of the road and, on the other side of the road, Toomer's Sports Shop had continued to attract the young and fit of Southampton's population. Sadly, neither firm exists today and London Road has been virtually taken over by estate agents and building societies.

London Road, looking north, *c.* 1960. At the end of the Second World War Lloyds Bank was the only building that remained standing between Waterloo Terrace and Carlton Crescent. Rebuilding of the area did not begin until the early 1960s. The photograph shows the first of the new buildings taking shape. That building was called Halpin House, after Halpin's of Hampshire, an electronics company that also sold radios and televisions and had a showroom on the ground floor. The upper floors of the building were let out as offices. In the middle distance can be seen the old National Provincial Bank Building, on the corner of Carlton Crescent, which was in the process of major renovations when the photograph was taken. (City Heritage Services)

London Road, looking north, 1997. London Road looks entirely different now. All building was complete by the middle of the 1960s. Among those occupying some of the modern new shops were Raymond, the ladies' hairdresser, Jill Ford's shoe shop, Atherley dry cleaners, Hamilton Electronics and the London Road post office. The occupants of the shops have changed over the years but the biggest difference is in the number of cars parked by the side of the road: another indication of Southampton's traffic problems.

Mount Pleasant Road, *c.* 1960. The photograph shows the northern side of Mount Pleasant Road, between Bevois Valley Road and Mount Pleasant School. While the southern side of the road was allowed to remain more or less intact, the northern side of the road was almost completely demolished in the 1960s. Apart from Osmond, the glass merchant, next door to the Crown and Sceptre public house, all the houses were privately occupied but were old and in need of extensive and expensive refurbishment. (Southampton Archives Services)

Mount Pleasant Road, 1997. The old houses on the northern side of Mount Pleasant Road were pulled down in about 1968 but not replaced by new housing, as some would have liked. Instead, the land was given over to the industrial units that stand behind the mature trees that now border the road. The southern side of the road, however, looks much the same as it did thirty years ago. The road itself once provided a convenient short cut from Portswood to Northam Bridge and back, without having to negotiate the notorious Six Dials. Now it is almost traffic free owing to its speed humps and chicanes.

Portswood Road, *c.* 1949. Like Bevois Valley Road and Banister Road, Portswood Road received its name from one of the large estates in the area. Portswood Lodge, built at the end of the eighteenth century, was one such estate and Portswood House, which was built a bit further south at about the same time, was another. The land from both estates, although belonging to different families, was sold for development in the first and second decades of the twentieth century. The part of Portswood Road in the photograph was developed mainly in the 1920s and has been known as Portswood Broadway for years. The photograph shows the old tram lines still in existence, although the nos 11, 12, 13 and 14 buses had taken over the old tramcar routes. (Southampton Archives Services)

Portswood Road, 1997. The profile of the buildings in Portswood Road looks much the same as it did nearly fifty years ago. However, many of the shops have changed hands over the years and there is an abundance of ubiquitous 'high street' shops such as Boots the Chemist and Woolworths. However, many small shops still operate in the road and add interest to a very busy shopping centre for local people. Parking has been restricted along the road and there are fewer buses today, so the scene looks a lot quieter than it did in 1949.

Portswood Road, *c*. 1955. Portswood Road once boasted two cinemas: the Palladium, seen in the photograph, and the Broadway, which was further down the road on the opposite side. The Palladium opened in 1913 and was a favourite Saturday evening venue for many local people. With Holmes' sweet shop next door to the cinema, the formula was right for a pleasant evening out. Sadly, the old cinema closed in May 1958 and was replaced by a Fine Fare supermarket. The Broadway still exists but became a bingo hall in 1963. (Veal Collection)

Portswood Road, 1997. Portswood Library still stands next door to the site of the old Palladium Cinema. The building is still a supermarket, but has not belonged to Fine Fare for many years. Portswood Junction, the point from which both photographs were taken, changed in the 1980s when St Denys Road was diverted around the back of the public house that is now called the Pickled Newt, but was then the Belmont Hotel. As with all modern-day pictures of Southampton, traffic lights predominate in the scene.

Portswood Road, *c.* 1958. The part of Portswood Road between Portswood Junction and Swaythling High Road was not a busy shopping centre like the rest of the road. Although mostly residential properties, there were also many small shops and businesses along the road. The photograph shows how the road looked in about 1958 when Brook Terrace dominated the corner of Belgrave Road. According to the 1962 street directory, Miss Alma Bailey owned the confectioner's shop at no. 1, Donald Ackford lived at no. 2, Mrs Baker was in no. 3, Charles Mintram lived in no. 4, Samuel Culmer had no. 5 and F.T. Lloyd resided at no. 6. (Southampton Archives Services)

Portswood Road, 1997. Brook Terrace was demolished in about 1969. The shop and the houses were very old indeed and uneconomical to maintain and repair. The site was given over to used-car dealers and several have since occupied the site. In this photograph, Hughes Motor Company occupies the left-hand side of the site, while the right-hand side is occupied by Belgravia Car Sales.

Portswood Road, *c.* 1970. When horse-drawn trams were introduced to Southampton, a depot where the horses could be fed, groomed and sheltered was established at Portswood Junction. Before long the horse-drawn trams gave way to electric trams and the depot was adapted accordingly. The trams stopped running in 1949 and the depot was later adapted to become the Portswood bus depot. The old building was eventually demolished and replaced by an open-air parking ground and garage, which belonged to Southampton Corporation Transport. Those who can remember the old tram depot must surely remember the old Portswood police station, which stood next door. (Southampton Archives Services)

Portswood Road, 1997. Southampton Corporation Transport became Citybus in the late 1980s when all of the country's public transport was privatized. The remaining garage buildings of the old bus depot, although not that old, were demolished and the site, while still remaining a bus depot, was planted with trees. The buses can no longer be seen from the main road because of the trees, but the depot is still there, serving as a reminder of over 100 years of public transport.

Portswood Road, *c.* 1965. Look at the 1965 prices of the cars on the front lot of the old Portswood Lodge – but don't forget that people were earning a lot less then than they do now! Portswood Lodge, otherwise known as Castle Lodge, was built in the late 1770s as an entrance to the old Portswood House. In the early part of the twentieth century it had a blacksmith's shop attached to it; that was removed in the 1930s. A Grade II listed building, it has survived the many changes in the area, even a proposal that it should be demolished, but protest from local residents put that idea to one side. (City Heritage Services)

Portswood Road, 1997. After it had been abandoned as a private dwelling in 1964, the small but elegant building suffered the ignominy of being used as a used-car dealer's premises, a blight that it had to endure for nearly thirty years. In the middle 1990s, however, the building was taken over as office accommodation and sympathetically restored to how it must have looked when first built in the 1850s.

Royal South Hants Hospital, *c*. 1950. The Royal South Hants Hospital was established on its present site in 1838. The hospital was extended over the years to include new wings in the 1850s. The chapel, seen on the left, was also added in the 1850s with funds from two local benefactors whose names have long since been forgotten. The nurses' home, on the right of the building, was damaged by bombs during the blitz. It stood empty for a while before being rebuilt to become habitable once more. In those days the address of the hospital was Fanshawe Street; the buildings stood on the corner of Fanshawe Street and Exmoor Road. (City Heritage Services)

Royal South Hants Hospital, 1997. The hospital was expanded greatly in recent years with a radiotherapy unit being added in 1970 and an outpatients' centre in 1986. Fanshawe Street barely exists any more, Exmoor Road has all but gone, and the hospital buildings stretch from Graham Road to Lyon Street. The old nurses' home has been demolished to become a staff car park; the only thing that serves as a reminder of how things were is the old chapel, which is now used as a storehouse.

The Sports Centre, c. 1955. Originally inspired by and later brought to fruition by Alderman Sydney Kimber, the Sports Centre was formally opened by the Duke and Duchess of Kent in 1938. Built on waste ground to the north of the town, the Sports Centre boasted several football pitches, tennis courts, a running track with a sports arena in the centre, a boating lake, a paddling pool, bowling greens, a putting course and, above all, a sports pavilion where refreshments could be had. An eighteen-hole golf course, complete with clubhouse, was laid out to the north of the Sports Centre. (Southampton Archives Services)

The Sports Centre, 1997. The Second World War slowed down the progress of the site as a comprehensive sports arena for the whole of Southampton's population, but since the war that population has expanded dramatically. All the facilities are still available and used fully. The pavilion, however, became a genuine public house in the 1980s, rather than just a licensed sports pavilion, and the view from there in 1997 shows how the trees have matured over the years. The park bench still exists!

Wide Lane, *c.* 1960. Looking towards Westfield Corner, Brown's Farm on the left had stood at the junction of Wide Lane and Mansbridge Road for many years. The photograph shows the farm being demolished to make way for road improvements. Opposite the farm, about where the Morris Minor is, stood the shop of Swaythling Antique Galleries and behind that was The Grange, an old manor house where Richard Cromwell is reputed to have stayed. Both buildings were demolished in the 1960s after remaining empty and derelict for years. (Southampton Archive Services)

Wide Lane, 1997. The site of Brown's Farm remained vacant for several years before being redeveloped when Grange Court, the present-day block of flats, was built. The road was widened, opening up the view towards Westfield Corner, and traffic at the dangerous junction of Wide Lane and Mansbridge Road was assisted by the construction of a roundabout. The sites of Swaythling Antique Galleries and The Grange are still vacant.

TO THE WEST

BLECHYNDEN, FREEMANTLE,
SHIRLEY AND MILLBROOK

Blechynden Terrace, 1954. Seen from the entrance to Central station, this area, between Commercial Road and the main railway line, was badly bombed during the blitz. A solitary, emergency pub had been erected on the site of the Station Hotel, but the rest of the area was still in ruins. In the foreground of the photograph is an advertisement for the Co-operative Society, stating 'You'll Save Far More in 1954 by Shopping at your Co-op Store', while St Peter's Church is in the background together with the Gaumont Cinema (now the Mayflower Theatre). (Veal Collection)

Blechynden Terrace, 1997. The whole area has altered drastically since 1954. The few buildings that remained after the bombing were demolished in 1967, being redeveloped in ugly concrete on a par with the Tricorn in Portsmouth. The Prince of Wales once described such concrete buildings as 'carbuncles on the face of the earth'.

Church Street, Shirley, 1964. Church Street was a road of varied housing styles dating back to the early part of the nineteenth century. Many public houses and small shops enjoyed a profitable business here until the early 1960s when the city planners decided to demolish the whole lot, apart from the few hundred yards that now lead into Shirley High Street. Reginald Dear's small grocery shop was just one of the many casualties of the mass demolition of the area. (Southampton Archives Services)

Church Street, Shirley, 1997. Church Street now consists of several blocks of 1960s-style flats. In fact, it is now impossible to drive a car the whole length of Church Street because it has changed so much in the past thirty years. Some of the original buildings remain at the junction with Shirley High Street, and St James' Church, after which Church Street was named, still exists at the top end of the street.

Commercial Road, looking west, *c.* 1953. Like the rest of the area around the Central station, Commercial Road was badly hit by German bombs during the war. Some buildings remained standing, albeit in a ruined state; the photograph shows buildings between Central Station Road and Sidford Street being taken down to make way for a second-hand car sales lot. The Hilltop Inn, in the middle distance, was allowed to continue in business for several more years, as were the handful of restaurants and cafés that were between the pub and Four Posts Hill. (Veal Collection)

Commercial Road, looking west, 1997. All the remaining buildings in the area were demolished in the early 1970s and replaced by the present-day Nelson Gate office block. The office block is set back from the road and screened by trees, which makes the whole scene look much more pleasant. On the right-hand side is another block of modern offices, erected in the early 1990s on a site that had seen many uses over the years, including that of a boot manufacturer, a chartered accountant and, latterly, a DIY store.

Crown Street, *c.* 1964. Narrow Crown Street, in the Shirley area of the city, received its name from the Crown Hotel, a public house on the corner of Shirley High Street. It is now hard to imagine that streets such as this, full of shops and houses, once existed so near main thoroughfares. Tatchell's Café was always popular with shoppers, being so close to the main Shirley shopping area. Other needs were catered for by Charles Malizia, the turf accountant with premises at the same address. When the photograph was taken, Mr Malizia had taken over the larger part of the building, while the café had become smaller and had been renamed the Coral Restaurant. (Southampton Archives Services)

Crown Street Shirley, 1997. The pub on the corner is now called Tramways but the name of the street remains as a reminder of how things were. Although Crown Street still exists, it no longer runs from Shirley High Street to Victor Street. When the area was redeveloped in the middle of the 1960s, the street received a 'kink', which put it nearer to parallel Redcar Street. Commercial premises now straddle what was Crown Street, while the betting shop and café sites are now used as parking for Lloyds Bank.

Four Posts Hill, *c.* 1950. In 1950 Four Posts Hill was on a busy road leading to Shirley, Millbrook and all other points to the west. The traffic problem was nowhere near as bad then as it is today, but the flow of traffic warranted the use of traffic lights at the busy four-point junction. On the hill to the right are the ruins of private houses that were destroyed in the blitz, while in the centre is part of a row of shops that escaped the bombing. (Veal Collection)

Four Posts Hill, 1997. Although the road is not as congested as it was, mainly because of the construction of Mountbatten Way in the late 1970s, Four Posts Hill is still a very busy traffic junction. The old traffic lights have long since been replaced by a mini-roundabout, the bomb sites are now occupied by new private dwellings, while the remains of the row of shops were demolished in the 1980s to make way for Anglo-City House, a block of modern offices.

Millbrook Road, 1945. The main road into the town from the west, being relatively close to the banks of the River Test, was seen as being a potential landing ground for enemy troops during the Second World War. As with many other similar sites, the area was lined with anti-tank 'dragons' teeth' to resist any invasion and a solitary 'knife rest' blocked the road into the city, although that did not deter the solitary cyclist in the photograph. Millbrook Road was a relatively quiet road in those days; the houses in the photograph had not long been erected as suburban dwellings when their view was obstructed by concrete blocks. (City Heritage Services)

Millbrook Road, 1997. Many of the buildings in Millbrook Road were demolished in the late 1960s so that the increasingly busy road could be widened. The junction of Millbrook Road, Wimpson Lane and Redbridge Road, just to the west of the photograph, was replaced by a roundabout in the 1950s, but the volume of traffic was so great that the roundabout was later replaced by a flyover. The road was widened to two lanes in each direction when the flyover was built but the houses, being a little way off the main road, managed to survive the redevelopment.

Paynes Road, *c.* 1960. The photograph shows the view to the east from the footbridge leading from Millbrook Road to Millbrook station. To the left of the photograph are Freemantle Park and Paynes Road; on the junction of Paynes Road and Millbrook Road lies the Millbrook filling station, and on the right of the photograph Millbrook Road goes on up to Four Posts Hill. Just out of camera shot on the right was Vincent & Elliott's (later Cooper's) oast house. Disused for many years, the oast house found a new lease of life when it was taken over by Lawton & Wilson to become their new motorcycle showroom in the 1950s. (Veal Collection)

Paynes Road, 1997. Millbrook Road has been a virtual cul-de-sac since the late 1970s when Mountbatten Way was constructed. This present-day photograph shows Paynes Road going east in, more or less, the direction that it always has. The west-bound direction is a different story, however, because Paynes Road now runs under Mountbatten Way, the road that dominates the picture, to join Millbrook Road some way west of the original junction. Note the new flats that have been erected at the bottom of Paynes Road.

Shirley High Street, c. 1949. Shirley had existed as a small hamlet since before the Norman invasion in 1066. The hamlet grew and prospered quite separately from Southampton, even to the extent of having several manor houses, until 1895 when it was taken into the Borough of Southampton and became part of the town. Still called Shirley High Street, the main road through the old hamlet grew and grew until it became a major shopping and business centre for people who lived in the area. The Southampton tramway system was extended to Shirley in 1879, thus giving it a permanent connection with the rest of the town. The last Southampton tramcar ran to the Shirley Depot in Park Street in 1949. (City Heritage Services)

Shirley High Street, 1997. The first impression that you get from the modern-day photograph is that the street hasn't changed much at all. It is only when you look closer that you see that the tram lines have disappeared, yet another set of traffic lights has been added and there is much more traffic on the road. Notice also the absence of the shop blinds that used to be so common. Winter & Worth, the highly respected bespoke tailors, had their premises on the corner of Shirley High Street and Shirley Avenue for many years. The building is now occupied by the Halifax Building Society.

Windermere Avenue, *c.* 1955. At the end of the Second World War many Southampton people had to be rehoused. At first 'prefabs' were erected in various parts of the town and eventually these were replaced by permanent dwellings. Millbrook was one of the principal areas for redevelopment: what had been cabbage fields suddenly became homes. The first phase was in about 1951 when Cheviot Avenue was built, the second phase came in 1953 when the Kendal Avenue area was completed, and the final phase was in about 1955 when Windermere Avenue and its environs were finished. (City Heritage Services)

Windermere Avenue, 1997. The scene in 1997 looks more permanent than that in 1955. More building took place in the years following the opening of Windermere Avenue so that today it contains high-rise flats and small, local shops. Many of the houses on the estate were built of preformed concrete slabs and put together in a matter of days. They looked nice when they were new. They had lots of accommodation but they were so cold! The only heating was an open fire in the living room, which was also meant to provide hot water via an inefficient back boiler. I am sure things are better in these enlightened times.

ACROSS THE RIVER

BITTERNE AND WOOLSTON

Bitterne Road, looking east, *c.* 1965. This part of Bitterne Road is in Bitterne Manor, named after the old manor house that once stood in grounds on the left of the photograph. Although the road looks very quiet, with a solitary van driving along it, at peak times the road was very busy indeed. Just a bit further along the road, where it meets Athelstan Road and Bullar Road, was a notorious roundabout which served to snarl up traffic entering the city in the mornings and leaving the city in the evenings. Many people will remember 'Tiny' Dyer, the 6-ft plus traffic-duty policeman whose job it was to keep the traffic moving at peak times. He kicked many a car – including mine! (Southampton Archives Services)

Bitterne Road, looking east, 1997. This part of Bitterne Road is still busy at peak times but has been improved by the road-widening scheme and, further along, the introduction of traffic lights where the roundabout used to be. The mature trees on the left of the photograph hide the neat apartment building that was built on the site of the old Bitterne Manor in the 1950s. When the site was being excavated during the building of the apartment block, many Roman artefacts were found there because the old manor house had in fact stood on *Clausentum*, an ancient Roman settlement.

Bitterne Road, looking west, *c*. 1965. This photograph must have been taken at a time other than the rush hour because the traffic is so light. Traffic in this part of Bitterne Road, looking across Northam Bridge towards the city, tailed back from the Six Dials one-way system – a distance of almost a mile. Northam Bridge was about ten years old when the photograph was taken and, although the new bridge was infinitely better than the one it replaced, the approach roads to the bridge were still as they were years before. (Southampton Archives Services)

Bitterne Road, looking west, 1997. The view towards the city in 1997 does not look much different from that of 1965. New industrial units have been erected on the right-hand side of the road but, like so many other streets in Southampton, new traffic lights have been installed to control traffic turning into the new industrial estate on the right. Traffic is still a problem, although maybe not the problem that it was. Between the junction of Athelstan Road and what was the Six Dials there are at least eight sets of traffic lights, including those for pedestrian crossings, so progress is still slow.

Bitterne Road, looking east, *c.* 1971. The 'Y' junction of Bitterne Road and Bursledon Road was a familiar sight to many people but negotiating a motor car through it could be hazardous and confusing. This part of Bitterne Road was once known as Bitterne High Street because it was the main thoroughfare for Bitterne village. The village was incorporated into the Borough of Southampton in 1920 and Bitterne High Street changed to Bitterne Road. Dating back to the early years of the nineteenth century, the Red Lion public house has been the subject of many photographs over the years. (Southampton Archives Services)

Bitterne Road, looking east, 1997. Bitterne Road and its notorious 'Y' junction was a major traffic problem in the city. In the 1980s, therefore, this part of Bitterne Road became a pedestrianized shopping precinct and the roads to the east were diverted around it. Lances Hill, which led from the west to the main shopping area, was bypassed, and Pear Tree Avenue and West End Road were widened. Several sets of traffic lights were inevitably installed. The shopping precinct, however, enhances the environs of this thriving community, which still retains a village atmosphere.

Bursledon Road, looking west, *c.* 1970. This photograph shows the view into Bitterne Road from one leg of the notorious 'Y' junction. In the middle distance the shops in Bitterne Road can be clearly seen, as can the spire of Bitterne Church, otherwise known as the Church of the Holy Saviour. Burden's service station, seen on the left of the photograph, was still open, while, in competition on the right-hand side of the road was the Red Lion filling station. Thereafter, on the right-hand side of the road, were private dwellings from Ernest Wheeler's house at no. 3 until Alex Egerton's grocer's shop at no. 81, on the corner of Bath Road. (Southampton Archives Services)

Bursledon Road, looking west, 1997. Although the shops in Bitterne Road can still be seen, otherwise the view along Bursledon Road is quite different. This part of the road is no longer used much by traffic, having been bypassed to the north. The trees around Bitterne Church have matured so much that they now almost obscure the spire from view. The two filling stations became redundant when the road was bypassed, and the private houses on the right-hand side of the road were replaced by a kitchen furniture shop and a car salesroom when the area was redeveloped.

Glen Road, *c.* 1980. Running from Swift Road to Weston Grove Road, in the Woolston area of the city, Glen Road typifies the smaller residential areas on the east of the River Itchen. The terrace of cottages seen in this photograph was built in Victorian times when Woolston was a small village on the east bank of the River Itchen. Like Bitterne village, Woolston was taken into the Borough of Southampton in 1920 and, because the main link with the rest of the city was by way of the Floating Bridge, the district developed in its own way until the opening of the Itchen Bridge in 1977. (Taunton's College)

Glen Road, 1997. Much of the development of this part of Woolston started in the 1920s and 1930s. Glen Road was one of the few original streets to remain after redevelopment. It was not invulnerable, however, to the planners' designs and the old buildings were torn down in the early 1980s to make way for more modern dwellings. Apart from the up-to-date appearance of the new buildings, the street looks much the same as it always did.

Obelisk Road, *c.* 1953. Confined mostly to privately owned residential properties, one outstanding feature of Obelisk Road, in Woolston, was Lankester & Crook's emporium, where their registered office was located. Lankester & Crook were established in the latter years of the nineteenth century and had many shops on the eastern side of the River Itchen, as well as in Shirley and Portswood. They were ironmongers who also sold wines and spirits, grocery items, meat, stationery, china and glass, and tobacco. The solitary, white-topped pump outside the premises in Obelisk Road was for the delivery of paraffin as part of their hardware service. (Southampton Archives Services)

Obelisk Road, 1997. The old premises of Lankester & Crook are the only ones still recognizable as belonging to the company: all other premises owned by the company were either demolished or altered beyond recognition. The Obelisk Road premises were split into several smaller units when the company ceased trading in the 1960s. At the time of writing two of the units are empty, awaiting new lessees, one is used by a printer as a printing workshop, while another unit is used as a haberdashery.

Portsmouth Road, looking west, *c*. 1965. The lower end of Portsmouth Road in Woolston was very busy in its heyday. The road led down to the Floating Bridge Hard and was used daily by many people from both sides of the River Itchen. Many small shops, cafés and businesses occupied the buildings on each side of the road. Since 1913 the Woolston Picture House, which can be seen halfway down on the right-hand side of the road, was a major attraction. However, the end of the road near to the Floating Bridge Hard was badly damaged during the wartime air raids on the nearby Supermarine aircraft works, so few people still lived there when the war was over. (Gallaher Collection)

Portsmouth Road, looking west, 1997. Apart from the inevitable set of traffic lights, the scene in 1997 has altered little, but new houses were built in the early 1980s on the sites of the bombed buildings. They can be seen in the middle distance. The lower end of Portsmouth Road is seldom used now: there is nowhere for the traffic to go since the Itchen Bridge opened in 1977. The Woolston Picture House building still exists but it closed as a cinema in 1973 and is now a bingo hall.

Victoria Road, *c.* 1948. Running from Portsmouth Road to Foreshore Road, Victoria Road has always been the main shopping area for the people of Woolston. Much of the road was taken up with residential properties but the end near the junction of Portsmouth Road boasted many shops. Such shops ranged from Mrs Jaconelli's greengrocer shop on the corner of Lake Road to Lankester & Crook's enormous general store that occupied nos 15, 17, 19 and 21. The photograph shows that bicycles are predominant in the scene just after the end of the Second World War. The occasional car can be seen, but parking was not a problem. (City Heritage Services)

Victoria Road, 1997. Rebuilding after the war commenced in the 1950s and included the addition of a brand-new Woolworth's store near the corner of Portsmouth Road. The London Arms public house was rebuilt at the same time. Lankester & Crook's store, which disappeared in the 1960s, had other uses before it was replaced by the modern building that now houses the Co-op 'Stop and Shop' supermarket. Parking is more of a problem. Cars are allowed to park on either side of the road (if they can find a space) and traffic is still expected to flow through the rows of parked cars. Not easy, even on a Sunday!

ACKNOWLEDGEMENTS

Researching the information for this book has made me realize just how much Southampton has changed since I was born in the city in 1939. Many people of my generation have shown an interest in the project and, while I cannot thank them all individually, their help has been invaluable.

However, several people must be singled out for recognition of their significant contribution because, if it were not for those people, this book might never have been written.

Mr Veal was a keen local historian and photographed many Southampton scenes in the 1950s, 1960s and 1970s. When he died in 1977, his widow donated his splendid collection of photographs to the Southampton Archives Services. Sadly his widow passed away a few years ago and I have been unable to track down her successors. Where I have used a 'Veal' photograph, I have acknowledged it as being part of the Veal Collection. The collection is too good to languish in an archive: it deserves to be shown to the public at large. I thank Mr Veal for his foresight in photographing the city during that period.

Andrew George of the Southampton Archives Services merits a special mention because he went out of his way to help me track down obscure photographs of many parts of the city. Many of the photographs were commissioned by the City Council and are catalogued in the archives as SC/H2/xxx. The hundreds of photographs in the collection can be viewed by the public at the Southampton Archive Services office in the Civic Centre.

Alastair Arnott of the Southampton City Heritage Services showed a keen interest in the project. He also went out of his way to help me with several old photographs in the collection that he safeguards in Melbourne Street.

Other contributors worthy of a mention are Ron Williams, both for photographs and information, and Ron Norris for keeping me informed of what was happening east of the River Itchen. My old friends Ken Judd and Tony Short deserve a mention for searching their memories for answers to the many questions that I asked them regarding the years when we were all growing up in the city.

Debbie Corner of the Royal Navy Submarine Museum in Gosport has to be congratulated for tracking down the name of the submarine that appears in the illustration on page 64. Likewise my thanks go to Gill Allwood of the Southampton Community Health Council for giving me information on the history of Southampton's hospitals.

Thanks also to my wife Joyce and my friend Ralph Downton for reading my manuscript and pointing out missing words, transposed words and other typographical errors.

Where I have been unable to locate the precise owners of photographs, after taking all reasonable efforts to find them, I have acknowledged them simply as belonging to the Gallaher Collection. Photographs without any acknowledgement at all are those that I took myself; therefore the copyright is mine.

Should I have inadvertently infringed anyone's copyright, then I apologize. In every case I did my best to find copyright owners, but some just eluded me completely.

Tony Gallaher, September 1998